ERIC CLAPTON:
A Biography

ERIC CLAPTON:
A Biography

John Pidgeon

VERMILION
London Melbourne Sydney Auckland Johannesburg

Vermilion & Company

An imprint of the Hutchinson Publishing Group

17–21 Conway Street, London W1P 6JD

Hutchinson Publishing Group (Australia) Pty Ltd
16–22 Church Street, Hawthorne, Melbourne, Victoria 3122

Hutchinson Group (NZ) Ltd
32–34 View Road, PO Box 40–086, Glenfield, Auckland 10

Hutchinson Group (SA) Pty Ltd
PO Box 337, Bergvlei 2012, South Africa

First published 1976
Revised edition 1985
© John Pidgeon 1976, 1985

Set in Linotron Ionic

Printed and bound in Great Britain by Anchor Brendon Ltd,
Tiptree, Essex

British Library Cataloguing in Publication Data
Pidgeon, John
    Eric Clapton : a biography. — Rev. and
    updated ed.
    1. Clapton, Eric   2. Rock musicians —
    England – Biography
    I. Title
    787.6′1′0924   ML419.C58

    ISBN 0 09 160161 4

In memory of Jamie Jess

CONTENTS

ACKNOWLEDGEMENTS

Most of the interviews used in the book are my own, but I'm indebted to the editors of *Melody Maker*, *New Musical Express*, *Record Mirror* and *Rolling Stone*, and to Barbara Charone for additional material, as I am to Throat Music for permission to quote from 'Blues Power', 'Give Me Strength', 'Golden Ring', 'Layla' and 'Presence Of The Lord', and to E. C. Music for 'Ain't Going Down'. The late Alexis Korner was a great help with the background of British rhythm and blues, and thanks are also due to Chris Barber, Moira Bellas, Tom Dowd, Jeremy Fletcher, Hughie Flint, Roger Forrester, Hamish Grimes, John Gunnel, Philip Hayward, Dick Heckstall-Smith, Susan Hill, Glyn Johns, Paul Jones, Jim McCarty, Tom McGuinness, Ian McLagan, Ben Palmer, Paul Samwell-Smith, Dick Taylor, Mike Vernon, Helen Walters, Ron Watts, Chris Welch, Cliff White, Ron Wood, and, of course, Eric Clapton himself.

LIST OF ILLUSTRATIONS

INTRODUCTION

The electric guitar has been the lead instrument of rock ever since the music exploded across the Atlantic thirty years ago. And yet the lasting images from rock'n'roll's earliest years are of its singers: outrageous wild-eyed hell-raisers like Elvis Presley, Jerry Lee Lewis and Little Richard, tormented weaklings like Gene Vincent, dewy youths like Ricky Nelson. Others accompanied themselves on guitar, but though Chuck Berry, Buddy Holly and Eddie Cochran were later acknowledged as inspirational stylists, it wasn't their playing that made them popular at the time. All the same, many of the sounds that still echo from the fifties were created by guitarists, modest men who stood outside the spotlight, like Presley's Scotty Moore, Vincent's Cliff Gallup and Nelson's James Burton.

Before the sixties the guitarists' obscurity was broken by Duane Eddy in America and soon after by the Shadows' Hank Marvin in Britain, but other accomplished English players like Marty Wilde's Big Jim Sullivan and Mick Green of Johnny Kidd's backing group, the Pirates, were appreciated most by their peers. (More pointedly, Jimmy Page remained unknown outside the freemasonry of session men until his recruitment by the Yardbirds in 1966.)

The British groups boom which began with the appearance, low in the top thirty, of the Beatles' 'Love Me Do' at the end of 1962, and which dominated popular music in the mid-sixties, permanently altered the pattern of the solo singer supported by backing musicians and simultaneously shifted the balance of musical power across the Atlantic to the UK. The first great rock guitarists had been American, but within these British groups a new generation of guitarists emerged. Black music reasserted itself as the lifeblood of rock, although the musicians who learned from Chuck Berry, Bo Diddley, Muddy Waters, the three Kings, Otis Rush and the rest, were white.

The British rhythm and blues boom was at the core. The continual exploration of new sources of material, the freedom of the twelve-bar blues structure, the long sets performed in the expanding circuit of R&B clubs, and the insatiable enthusiasm of musicians and audiences alike, encouraged the development of the young guitarists' talents. They weren't all virtuosos, but there was an elite of guitar apprentices in those groups who learned well enough to divert the gaze of the crowd from the front men with the microphone to their fingers on the fretboard, whose own admirers packed tightly around their small space on stage and asked questions in the interval about solos and strings and styles. Those few were ultimately to earn their own fame and to raise the status of the guitarist from sideman to superman. They created a new idol in pop music: the guitar hero. And Eric Clapton was their prototype.

One

GOT R&B IF YOU WANT IT, BABE

The British rhythm and blues boom had unlikely and premature beginnings in the early fifties. Traditional jazz, as yet unabbreviated and still earnestly dedicated to the revival of New Orleans jazz, was gradually building up the popular momentum which would eventually bring about a trad boom at the start of the sixties.

Chris Barber, the music's leading popularizer, who played trombone and led a band with Ken Colyer, formed a small group within the band to play 'race music' (for which rhythm and blues became an inoffensive euphemism) during the interval. Barber's banjoist, Tony Donegan, played guitar and sang to the accompaniment of washboard percussion and double bass (played by Barber himself), and the popularity of these short sets prompted Barber to include two numbers by the group on his band's *New Orleans Joys* album in 1954. 'Rock Island Line' and 'John Henry' were released as a single late in 1955. The record lodged in the top twenty for the first seventeen weeks of 1956, made the American top ten (an unprecedented achievement for a British performer), turned Donegan – now Lonnie, in homage to his blues hero, Lonnie Johnson – into one of the most consistent hitmakers of the next years, and created Britain's first truly homegrown pop craze, skiffle.

Skiffle was archetypal youth club music; all it required was four kids, three chords, two secondhand acoustic guitars, a washboard for percussion, and a tea-chest bass with a broomhandle neck and a yard of string to plunk. The fad spread throughout the country, disenchanting the serious-minded jazzers who had inadvertently set it in motion and temporarily discouraging Chris Barber from experimenting with blues. Yet his original intention had indeed been to play blues. What went wrong was Donegan's voice, a high-pitched nasal whine that lent itself poorly to the songs Barber and he loved, although, according to Barber, Sonny Terry once mistook Donegan's recording of

'Leaving Blues' for Leadbelly.

The self-styled London Skiffle Centre was housed in the Roundhouse pub on the corner of Wardour Street and Brewer Street, W.1. Its Thursday evening sessions were taken over in 1955 by Alexis Korner, a blues enthusiast who had played in Barber's first amateur band in 1950, and Cyril 'Squirrel' Davies, a panel beater by day who had played banjo in a variety of skiffle groups and in Steve Lane's Southern Stompers, a traditional jazz band, but who developed an interest in blues which led him to take up twelve-string guitar and, subsequently, harmonica. Korner and Davies transformed the Skiffle Centre into the London Blues and Barrelhouse Club, where they played regularly to a small but committed audience of enthusiasts, who were encouraged to join in.

Although the trad boom's most obvious manifestation – a succession of hit singles by the best-known names – was delayed until the start of the sixties, Chris Barber was packing concert halls from the mid-fifties, and he used his popularity to spread the word about blues. His first venture was a tour with Big Bill Broonzy and Brother John Sellars in 1957, and its success prompted him to do the same with Sister Rosetta Tharpe, Sonny Terry and Brownie McGhee, and, crucially in 1958, with Muddy Waters. Although Waters failed to sell out St Pancras Town Hall on his only London appearance and upset a number of blinkered blues purists by his use of amplification (as Sister Rosetta Tharpe had done a year before), the effect of his visit on the key figures in the nascent British R&B movement was decisive.

After seeing Waters play in front of a Chicago audience a couple of months later in early 1959 – 'the most unbelievable experience ever' – Barber began to incorporate rhythm and blues material, especially Waters', into his band's repertoire, and his vocalist, Ottilie Patterson, was probably the first singer in Britain to perform what was to become the anthem of the R&B boom, '(I've Got My) Mojo Working'. But the traditional instrumentation of the Barber band lacked the bite and resonance of Waters' sound, and Barber eventually brought in Korner and Davies to play electric rhythm and blues with Ottilie Patterson for the final half hour of his band's set.

Korner and Davies, together with Long John Baldry, had been experimenting with amplification since Waters' visit and Davies had abandoned his guitar for a harmonica. The R&B sets with Ottilie Patterson were immediately popular, especially at the Marquee Club, then in Oxford Street, W.1., headquarters of the National Jazz Federation, run by Barber and Harold Pendleton; but they weren't entirely successful. Korner, though he later proved himself to be an inspirational bandleader and the father figure of British R&B, was a limited instrumentalist, while Davies interpreted his supporting role as a duel with Ottilie Patterson's voice. Barber dropped Korner and Davies, and by doing so virtually ended his association with rhythm and blues. Certainly he curtailed his own influence on the music's future in Britain, preferring to protect the reputation of true traditional jazz as a caravan of fancy-dressed charlatans peddled their watery trad like patent medicine to a gullible public. When he finally switched his band's instrumentation – bass guitar for double bass, lead guitar for banjo – and returned to R&B in 1964, he was unfairly branded as an opportunist.

Ironically, it was Barber's band manager, Phil Robertson, who persuaded Korner and Davies, already impressed by the Marquee crowd's response to their music, to form their own electric rhythm and blues band in 1961.

Blues Incorporated, as they called the group, was unique, which meant there were few places to play. The music was too earthy by half for pop promoters, its exponents eccentric and even elderly, and too loud and too close to rock 'n' roll for the jazz club circuit. The solution was straightforward, though hazardous. On 17 March 1962, Korner and Davies opened their own rhythm and blues club in premises known to Davies as an after-hours drinking den under the ABC teashop by Ealing Broadway underground station in west London.

There was little advertising apart from a few posters and a small ad in *Jazz News* which announced 'the most exciting event of the year ... [the] debut of Britain's first rhythm & blues band ... this Saturday & every Saturday:– 7.30 p.m.', but they hoped at least a few cognoscenti would turn up. The Ealing Club was packed on that first night. It was packed on each subsequent Saturday night too. Less than seven weeks after they opened the club, Blues Incorporated were booked into the first 'rhythm and blues night', the start of a long residency, at the Marquee.

The line-up of the band had by then already shifted from its original personnel, but similar aims held its musicians together: a love of the blues and a parallel hatred of trad's lifeless mummery. Most of the musicians had, in fact, played at one time or another in traditional jazz bands. The first line-up included vocalist Art Wood and Charlie Watts on drums, but by the summer Wood had left (to form the Art Wood Combo, later the Artwoods), Jack Bruce had joined as bassist and Ginger Baker had replaced Charlie Watts; Dick Heckstall-Smith was playing tenor sax, and there was a succession of pianists – Keith Scott, Dave Stevens, Johnny Parker. Besides Davies' vocals, Long

John Baldry would take a turn at the microphone, and so would
Mick Jagger.

Blues Incorporated's loosely structured sets at the Ealing Club
allowed other musicians to sit in and the club became a breeding
ground for R&B groups. Paul Jones (as P. P. Pond) would duet
with Brian Jones (who had chosen Elmo Lewis as a more
appropriate name for a blues guitarist), and the embryonic
Rolling Stones were regular visitors, as Dick Taylor, the group's
first bass guitarist who later founded the Pretty Things, recalls:
'We (himself, Jagger and Keith Richard) went down there and we
thought Alexis Korner's band was fantastic the first week, and
quite good the second week, but by the third week we thought it
was really a bit off – apart from Cyril Davies – and we thought,
"They're standing up there earning money for it; we'll try and
earn money for it." The stuff we were doing was different from
them anyway, and we thought we could do something. It finished
up with Brian Jones getting to know all us lot and we were
basically the Stones plus Ian Stewart. We were rehearsing all
this time in a pub in Broadwick Street, but the drummer never
used to turn up, and that's when Charlie Watts first appeared.'
The Stones made their first public appearance at the Marquee
on 12 July 1962, depping for Blues Incorporated who were
broadcasting on BBC radio's *Jazz Club*, and reappeared there
several times as an interval act before Barber and Pendleton
sacked them because, according to Barber, 'they weren't authentic enough – even then they'd gone into British R&B'.

During the summer months Blues Incorporated established a
following at the Marquee and a reputation which by August
provided rhythm and blues with its first press coverage, in
Melody Maker, where Chris Roberts praised this return of pop to
its roots.

'Take a trip to the Marquee Club on a Thursday night when
Alexis Korner and Cyril Davies are stomping along with Blues
Incorporated.

'That is, if you don't mind people standing on your head – the
club's popularity has to be seen, heard and felt to be believed.

'Their kind of music – using a line-up of guitar, harmonica
(amplified), sax, piano, bass and drums – is sure to put in a big
take-over bid in rock clubs and dance halls all over Britain.'

Later that month Korner himself, interviewed in the same
paper, stated, 'I think the music has a very strong future. In fact,
I believe it will be the next "big thing".

'The audience we get includes trad fans, modern fans, beat
fans, real R&B fans, and folk-music fans, and it includes most
age groups. All of them like to dance, and many twist themselves

to a standstill....

'And basically, whatever else we try to do, we are a dance band. We *want* to play for dancing. 'The point is, we are not following a popular trend. There's never been a band like this in Britain.'

Asked if he thought rhythm and blues could break trad's stranglehold, he replied, 'I don't think it can this year. But some time next year it may, if trad stays as it is, of course. I anticipate that there'll be a hell of a lot more R&B bands by the end of the year.'

Korner was right. Already, another West End jazz club, the Flamingo in Wardour Street, had introduced its own brand of rhythm and blues in place of modern jazz at Saturday's all-nighter sessions which attracted American servicemen on weekend leave, West Indians, and the first mods. And Georgie Fame and the Blue Flames topped the all-nighter bill for the first time in September 1962.

In November Cyril Davies left Blues Incorporated and adopted Screaming Lord Sutch's former backing group, the Savages, as his All-Stars, adding Long John Baldry and a female vocal trio, the Velvettes. Also by then the Manne-Hugge Blues Brothers had evolved from Manfred Mann and Mike Hugg's residency with a modern jazz quartet at a seaside holiday camp that summer.

As 1962 began, Acker Bilk's 'Stranger On The Shore' was at the top of the British charts, due to remain in the top twenty for some nine months. As one music journalist observed, 'Trad in 1962 is big business, with some fifty full professional bands based on London alone.' The BBC Light Programme's new *Trad Tavern* occupied two and three-quarter hours of air time every Saturday night, and there was even a BBC television series, *Trad Fad*, which was compered by Brian Matthew (from radio's *Saturday Club* and *Easy Beat*) and produced by Johnny Stewart, who, according to Matthew in his book, *Trad Mad*, 'had one ... order to give to the [studio] dancers. No beatniks and no weirdies! He wanted no one on the screen wearing jeans, and all the girls admitted had to wear skirts. He knew, of course, that in any jazz club you will always find some members of the great unwashed, with their bizarre clothes and off-beat habits, but he felt that they represented only a very small minority of jazz fans, and were completely unnecessary to his programme. "Jazz is still jazz," he said, "whether it is played on Salisbury Plain or the lounge of a luxury liner. But it is not enhanced by dingy surroundings and odd hangers-on. I want to prove to its detractors that it is a most interesting form of music, which does not have to be presented in dirt and discomfort. I have built a clean, bright set, and I want it filled with clean, bright people who enjoy jazz." '

Until chart success made it pop music and bands like Kenny Ball's (with seven hits in two years) appeared at the London Palladium, trad had remained essentially a club music, both ignored by and aloof from the conventional pop venues. A network of clubs had spread across the country, sometimes in established premises, but more frequently in pub annexes. For a while trad convinced a lot of punters that it was a vital alternative to the hit parade. 'Rock fans,' opined Brian Matthew, 'require more from the music than a sheer jungle beat. They want original ideas all the time.' Yet trad rapidly lost all relevance to either jazz or anything more traditional than Tin Pan Alley's bandwagoneering.

By August 1962 bandleader Alan Elsdon was condemning the 'agents and promoters [who] have flooded the jazz clubs with inferior bands', while Mike Cotton, who later converted his Mike Cotton Jazzmen into the R&B-oriented Mike Cotton Sound by switching instruments and hairstyles, admitted, 'There is no doubt the big boom is on the wane.'

Rhythm and blues was the universal remedy: a cure for dwindling club audiences, an elixir for tired musicians, and ultimately a shot in the arm for the music industry (though not until it had recovered sufficiently from its obsession with the Beatles and the Northern groups to bend an ear to its own back yard).

The motives of the emergent movement of R&B musicians spanned the scale of 'authenticity' from the bigoted self-styled purists, who were generally ex-jazzers, to the enthusiastic ragbag of the Rolling Stones. In an interview conducted early in 1963 by the Stones' then manager, Giorgio Gomelsky, which appeared later in *Jazzbeat*, Mick Jagger suggested, 'A lot of the stuff that we do, like the Chuck Berry numbers, are not awfully different, at least from the singing point of view [from rock 'n' roll]; they are in fact very similar to a lot of the Jerry Lee Lewis numbers, sort of wild; I mean there are differences between a rock number and a Muddy Waters number but they are not really so marked. Jerry Lee Lewis is a blues-influenced performer and Muddy Waters is a blues performer. There isn't really much difference between a good rocker or a white R&B singer and a Negro R&B artist.' Nevertheless, when the group's formation for their first appearance had been announced the year before, he had been careful to point out that the Stones weren't 'a rock 'n' roll outfit'.

Brian Jones outlined his own attitude in the same interview: 'If you ask some people why they go for R&B you get pretentious answers. They say that in R&B they find "an honesty of expression, a sincerity of feeling", and so on, for me it's merely the sound ... I used to play Dixieland [i.e. trad] but it never really excited me. My tastes are becoming more and more basic, really.'

Whatever their intentions, one ambition was absent from the musicians' considerations as they formed the first British rhythm and blues groups: the question of the commercial viability of their music simply did not arise. According to Manfred Mann vocalist Paul Jones, 'I remember Manfred looking over the top of the piano, pushing his glasses up his nose, and saying, "We're going to be bigger than the Shadows!" And I thought, This guy's crazy – I didn't think anybody was going to listen to R&B, not in any numbers. Earlier Brian Jones had said he was going to start a band with Keith Richard and did I want to be singer? I said, "Look, Brian, you're wasting your time. Nobody's going to listen to our music. You can forget that. It's nice to play occasionally, but quite frankly you're being wildly optimistic." So I turned it down! In some ways that was a shame, but there'd never have been a Rolling Stones if I'd joined instead of Mick Jagger.'

And Tom McGuinness, who invited Eric Clapton to join his first band, the Roosters, recalls, 'The idea of there being a real commercial market for what we were doing just didn't strike us. We were doing it really – it sounds corny now in this cynical age – but we were doing it just because we loved playing rhythm and blues. We never thought we could do more than earn a couple of quid a night out of doing it.' The Roosters' pianist, Ben Palmer, felt the same: 'There weren't any commercial reasons that you could form a band for of that kind. It used to be you'd get enough money for a brown ale and a packet of crisps and we'd walk home. We used to walk home from some place where we used to play regularly – some buffalo lodge or something like that in the back of a pub – we used to walk home to Tom's house and we didn't ever seem to have any money at all. When we did get paid, what we got was never enough to pay for getting there. Nor was anybody else, as far as we knew, getting paid anything. The idea of it offering a professional wage really didn't occur to me, and I doubt if it occurred to the others. Apart from the fact that we liked the music, there were certain signs that people in general might find it acceptable, but I don't think we believed that strong enough to feel any sense of crusading. If it cost you two or three quid for the week-end to get to the rehearsal and sleep in Tom's house and hitchhike home or something, it seemed a perfectly reasonable exchange for the fun that you'd had at rehearsal; and when it came to doing the jobs, you had to contribute money for the petrol to get there. It didn't seem unjust or anything. We could still be playing in a buffalo lodge in the back of a pub in Kingston if nothing had happened. It wouldn't have been disappointing or surprising to us, I don't think.'

The Roosters were one of several early British R&B bands which folded before rhythm and blues took hold on anything more than a parochial scale. Apart from isolated strongholds in a few other cities (notably Manchester's Twisted Wheel, Sheffield's Mojo club and the Club A GoGo in Newcastle) the rhythm and blues movement was centred almost exclusively on London, although the Roosters grew out of an attempt to form an R&B group in Oxford, as Ben Palmer explains. 'It started really with an attempt by Paul Jones to start an R&B band, and through Alexis Korner at Ealing we met Brian Jones, who lived in Cheltenham, which is not very far from Oxford. Then we advertised and got Tom McGuinness, and I don't think there was anybody else at all. I don't even remember a drummer, we didn't worry about that at all. It seemed so unlikely that you'd ever find the sort of drummer who wanted to sit there doing the sort of things that were required of him; there just weren't people like that about at all. We considered it a miracle that we'd met each other – I mean me and Paul Jones – let alone running into Brian. So we didn't even really put ourselves out to find a full band. I can't remember how we worded the advertisement in *Melody Maker*, but in the loosest possible way – and Tom showed up out of it. Then when Brian decided to stick with Mick Jagger, who he'd sat in with a lot at Ealing – a very wise decision – Tom got hold of Eric. As far as I remember, Tom's girlfriend was at art school with Eric, and all she knew about him was that he liked playing the guitar.'

By this stage – early 1963 – Paul Jones had quit too. Leaving the Roosters to their week-end rehearsals, he got a job in a Slough cinema on Saturday evenings covering top ten hits. Although his singing was less assured than his stage presence, he passed an audition with the Manne-Hugge Blues Brothers, who were about to become Manfred Mann. Since none of the remaining Roosters had ambitions to sing they were obliged to search for another front man. Tom McGuinness found an old school-friend, Terry Brennan. According to McGuinness, 'There weren't many singers in London that one came across who just wanted to sing rhythm and blues, which he did. He was quite good at impersonating Little Richard and people like that. Then we looked round for a bass player and drummer for ages. I can't even remember how we got the drummer. I do know that the big advantage he had was that he had a car. I think every band at that period had someone in the band who was in there because they had a car or a van. And we never found a bass guitarist. Everyone wanted to play Shadows and things like that if they'd got a bass guitar, so we never got one.'

McGuinness' girlfriend, who was studying fashion at Kingston Art College, had frequently mentioned a student who played acoustic blues in the cafeteria, but when Tom had suggested recruiting him to the Roosters she was doubtful that he would be willing to switch to electric. However, by the time McGuinness asked him to join the group, Clapton had already converted to a Hohner Kay, as played by Alexis Korner.

Although Clapton had not played in a group before he joined the Roosters, it was at once clear to the other members of the group that here was a rare gem – a rough diamond, maybe, but beneath the unpolished surface, flawless. He hadn't been playing long, a fact he confirmed in a 1966 *Melody Maker* interview. 'It was listening to Chuck Berry records that encouraged me to buy my first guitar at the age of sixteen. I taught myself a few chords and immediately joined a group called the Roosters.'

Born on 30 March 1945, he had been brought up in Ripley, Surrey, by his grandparents and developed an interest in records at school. But it was at art college that he, like so many of his contemporaries who were to become key figures in British rock in the sixties, began to explore the blues. 'I started out by liking [Buddy] Holly and Berry and people like that who were the first things I ever bought,' he once said, 'but then I'd read things on the back of album covers like, "Rock 'n' roll has its roots in blues," and stuff like that. And so I thought, what's that all about? I'll have to find out.' At college he 'started to play guitar and began listening to blues records all the time ... Muddy Waters, Big Bill Broonzy ... I could go on for hours. There's no point. Just the blues.'

According to Ben Palmer, 'he always seemed to have plenty to play even though it was quite clear to me he hadn't played very much guitar, because I'd worked in bands before – not those kind of bands, but I was used to listening to musicians for the first time and knowing whether there was going to be anything happening or not – but he always seemed to have enough to play in spite of being limited at the time.'

The Roosters were formed at the start of 1963, the year in which British rhythm and blues spread from its local base to national popularity, when the Rolling Stones made the top twenty for the first time in December. In the first week of the year, Mick Jagger, 'one of the newer faces on the R&B scene', was quoted as saying, 'It has got to move out of London. Only two or three clubs are making any money at the moment, and it has to spread to live. That's the only way it can become popular and retain its form at the same time.'

Apart from one appearance in Oxford, where Palmer was living, an undergraduate's twenty-first birthday party at Buxted in Sussex, and an interval spot at Uncle Bonnie's Chinese Jazz Club in Brighton, the Roosters' dozen or so public performances were confined to the West End (the Marquee and the Scene), Kingston (the Jazz Cellar club), and the flourishing Ricky Tick club circuit centred on Windsor. It wasn't until some time after the group broke up early in August that the number of venues for rhythm and blues grew sufficiently to support more than a handful of bands.

During the group's seven-month existence R&B was fighting a running battle with trad in the clubs; victory was won slowly in the face of determined resistance. Although some trad musicians like Dave Hunt and Pete Deuchar – a banjoist turned rhythm and bluesman, who told *Melody Maker* in February 1963, 'I changed from trad because I felt I was not having freedom of expression. We seemed to be playing the same old tunes to the same old people, and nobody was getting a kick out of it' – were keen to accept rhythm and blues, others like bandleader Micky Ashman scorned the new music, describing it as 'just a load of rubbish. Rhythm and blues? It's nothing but rock 'n' roll without the movements!' Certainly the Roosters' experience at Uncle Bonnie's Chinese Jazz Club was not uncommon among the early R&B bands, even if Terry Brennan's remedy was. 'We played there,' Tom McGuinness recalls, 'at that transitional period as trad was dying on its legs and the R&B thing was beginning, and we went down there and played the interval on trad night, and there were all these French students there who liked "le jazz hot" and Terry was moved to dive off stage and start a fight with them at one point because they were being so offensive about our amplifiers. The sight of an amplifier in a trad club was a bit like the Pope in certain parts of Belfast.' Uncle Bonnie's was one of the band's last gigs.

In fact, the Roosters were little better acquainted with amplification than their audiences. According to Ben Palmer, 'None of us had ever used amplification before, and so all those problems about not being able to hear each other and the audience saying it was too loud and that sort of thing we attributed solely to the manufacturers' shortcomings and we had no interest in it whatever. We didn't consider the electrical side of the sound as being anything more than just making the instruments louder. It didn't occur to us, I don't think.'

For several months after its formation the band rehearsed, mostly at the Prince of Wales at New Malden in Surrey, whenever they could all get together. This was not often since Palmer lived in Oxford and was generally broke, Clapton, having left college, was laying floors, Brennan was a painter and decorator and McGuinness was out of work. The first public appearance was at the Carfax Ballroom, Oxford, where they played a short spot during the interval at an Oxford Jazz Society evening. The band was paid five pounds. The repertoire leaned heavily on the standard Chuck Berry/Bo Diddley songbook, although Palmer's taste, like his piano style, veered singlemindedly towards Chicago in general and Otis Spann in particular, whose playing he copied slavishly. There were Little Richard and Fats Domino numbers, but also, as McGuinness puts it, 'rhythm and blues of that obscure sort that everyone liked at that period because you couldn't buy the records, so everyone thought, "How groovy! I've got a Billy Boy Arnold single, we'll do that." The obscurer the better. But there wasn't that much released over here, and you really had to ferret around to find it.' As well as Billy Boy Arnold's 'Here's My Picture, Baby', these obscurities included T-Bone Walker's 'Two Bones And A Pick' and Freddie King's 'Hideaway'. According to Palmer, 'We got a compromise together somehow. I hate to think what it sounded like really. I don't think it was that bad, but it was certainly pretty crude and rough and unpredictable.'

During the two and a half months that followed the Roosters' debut at the Carfax Ballroom and encompassed the group's public career, they performed only thirteen more gigs, the highest paid being those at the Ricky Tick clubs in Guildford, Reading and Windsor for which they received seventeen pounds ten shillings. The nearest they came to a residency was at the Jazz Cellar Club, Kingston, where they played on Wednesdays for three successive weeks. 'Can't be beat,' boasted the small ads, but in truth the sessions were poorly attended. The small audience, hardly a crowd, was almost entirely composed of people they knew.

The group's Ricky Tick club appearances attracted larger numbers, since these venues had quickly established a reputation among the growing number of R&B aficionados for booking good bands – the Stones had played there regularly in their early days – and fans would willingly pay to hear an unknown group. But generally, in spite of the approaching R&B boom, gigs were still scarce. 'It was difficult to get work,' McGuinness remembers, 'so it was difficult to make it worth-

while everyone's effort getting together to rehearse. And as we
averaged, say, thirty bob a gig, it wasn't very lucrative. No one
could give up work; I nearly had to start work. We did play at the
Marquee a couple of times, as support to Manfred Mann, which
was funny, but we had a row with him over the money. We said
we weren't being paid enough [£10] and we wouldn't play there,
which Manfred couldn't understand at all because he thought he
was doing us a favour by putting us on at the Marquee – which he
was – but we were young kids saying, "Hey, we want more than
that – it's not worth our while coming all the way to the Marquee
to play." ' (Whatever hard feelings arose between Manfred Mann
and the ungrateful Roosters had evidently been forgotten by
early 1964 when McGuinness replaced Dave Richmond on bass
guitar.) If the Roosters had stayed together even a few months
more, there would have been more places to play and a bigger
pool of musicians willing and able to play R&B – which would
have enabled them to find their missing bass player. As it was,
there were no rows, no unbridgeable musical differences, they
simply gave up. According to Ben Palmer, 'Alexis [Korner] and
Cyril [Davies] were certainly doing what we thought it was
possible to do without any mistake about it. We were appalled at
how good their band was and we didn't really seem to be getting
anywhere. And Eric certainly didn't intend to miss out. I'm not
saying he was ambitious, but I'm sure he felt he could be doing
better if he wasn't waiting around for us to find better fortune.
There was no question of anybody being the boss or making any
decisions – it was a very co-operative and happy-go-lucky affair –
and I think we just generally agreed that we weren't going to get
anywhere, and then he and Tom went off to Casey Jones; but
they didn't go off to Casey Jones and therefore leave the Roosters. Whatever the Roosters might have been was no longer even
a flimsy possibility. We just packed it in really.'

Palmer returned to Oxford, never expecting to see Eric Clapton again; Terry Brennan later sang with the Muleskinners; and
Clapton and McGuinness joined Casey Jones' Engineers. Jones
was a cocky, diminutive Liverpudlian in whose lap a recording
contract had landed while Merseybeat mania was addling the
brains of A&R men. He'd cut a single called 'One Way Ticket' as
Casey Jones and the Engineers. Since there were no Engineers
outside the recording studio, having only been added to the label
copy to provide a group identity, an outfit had to be rapidly
assembled for live performances.

As a step up the ladder for Clapton and McGuinness, backing
Casey Jones was mostly snakes: Clapton quit after the seventh
gig, McGuinness after the eighth. Musically unrewarding, the job

paid them little more than the Roosters, and on two occasions –
at Macclesfield Civic Hall and Manchester's Oasis – they were
obliged to provide appropriate backing for Polly Perkins as well.
'She wanted to do things like "Who's Sorry Now" and "Ain't
Misbehavin'",' recalls McGuinness. 'Eric and I attempted man-
fully to learn the chords, but failed totally. I can't imagine what
we played behind her, because I don't think either of us knew too
many chords. We really just wanted to boogie and play solos.'

Nevertheless, going out on the road to such distant venues did
make them feel like professional musicians for the first time, and
playing Chuck Berry numbers like 'Talkin' 'Bout You' was easy
work and might even have afforded some enjoyment were it not
for the presence of Casey Jones, who 'tended to sing sharp most
of the time, so it wasn't much pleasure accompanying him. And
he was a bit of a showbiz figure: he liked leaping around and the
adulation of the crowd – all twenty of them who turned up. It was
very short-lived. I turned up for a gig somewhere in town and
Eric didn't turn up for that one. I think I saw him later that night
wandering the streets of Soho and he said, 'No, no, I couldn't do
it any more.' So I said, 'I know what you mean, but he's still got
my amplifier.'

Two nights later on 10 October Casey Jones and the Engineers
played the Olympia Ballroom, Reading. Ben Palmer turned up
and helped McGuinness smuggle out his amplifier after the
show. Ironically, on that last night McGuinness got a raise. He
made four pounds.

Two

THE YARDBIRDS –
A SORT OF R&B GROUP

The Rolling Stones were undaunted, though unforgiving, after being dropped by the Marquee. By the end of 1962 the group had been reorganized by the arrival of Charlie Watts from Blues Incorporated and the replacement of Dick Taylor (whose ambition to study at the Royal College of Art, although it remained unfulfilled, overshadowed his desire to play bass guitar) by Bill Wyman into a line-up which, discounting manager Andrew Oldham's reduction of pianist Ian Stewart to the rank of roadie because he didn't look the part, survived longer than any other of the original R&B groups. They played regularly at a number of West End clubs, including an exceptionally unfortunate Monday night residency at the Flamingo where, according to the club's co-manager and compere John Gunnel, they died a death.

Then, early in 1963, Giorgio Gomelsky, a jazz writer and would-be impresario, started Sunday rhythm and blues nights at the Station Hotel, a popular jazz pub in Richmond, Surrey. He booked the Stones and organized the initial sessions of the Crawdaddy Club, as he called it, single-handed. Then he met Hamish Grimes, a young graphic designer, at a party and asked him to help out. 'About two weeks [after the club started],' Grimes recalls, 'I met Giorgio and he said, "Come down to the club," and that's when it went up doubling every week, every Sunday night. The word spread that it was something totally different. There was only a small group to whom mention of the Rolling Stones would have meant anything at all, and every single week the figures doubled until the place was absolutely full to capacity. It had a legal capacity of about three hundred and sixty or something, and we used to have nearly five hundred.' The organizers of a rival jazz club on Eel Pie Island, only a couple of miles up the Thames, choked on the laughter with which they had greeted the opening of the Crawdaddy Club, thought again and booked the group for a Wednesday night residency.

Within six months the club had to move premises from the

Station Hotel, which was due to be demolished, to the clubhouse at Richmond athletic ground. Gomelsky was soon forced to find another group as well. The Stones had an unwritten management agreement with him, which Brian Jones pressed him to reinforce in writing, but, according to Hamish Grimes, Gomelsky felt they wouldn't benefit from being 'tied down like a marriage'. On 28 April 1963, while Gomelsky was abroad, the precocious former Beatles PR assistant Andrew Oldham saw the group play at the club. Within a week he'd signed them to a management contract and a week later the Stones cut 'Come On', a Chuck Berry number that was not part of their repertoire, and 'I Wanna Be Loved' at Olympic Studios under Oldham's supervision.

Released as a single on 7 June, 'Come On' nudged into the top fifty at the end of the month, eventually climbing to No. 21 in September. The week the record entered the charts the music press reported that the group was the first act to join the Everly Brothers' British tour, due to open at the New Victoria, London, on 29 September.

By September, says Grimes, 'it just wasn't the same. We were all cheering for them when they were doing it, cheering away like mad – "Good old Stones!" – trying to get them bookings as well, going out flyposting with them in the bandwagon, sticking posters up all over the place, but we were cheering the death of the club in a certain sort of way. We didn't realize at the time that they were going to become so big that they would disappear, and eventually would start to get big-headed like everybody does, and they wouldn't be the same people any more. Instead of the agreement that we had before, that the money was split down the middle, it had to be pushed up and up and up. And finally they started to do television and they could get so many hundreds of pounds for playing at Manchester Town Hall or Birmingham Town Hall, and it would be "Sorry, they can't come down this Sunday". So we had to find somebody else very quickly and we dragged in the Yardbirds.'

The Yardbirds, epitome of British R&B, had grown out of a Kingston Art School band, the Metropolitan Blues Quartet, earlier in 1963. Keith Relf and Paul Samwell-Smith, together with a friend called Laurie Gain and a forgotten drummer, started out playing the interval spot at a Kingston jazz club. Samwell-Smith recalls, 'We'd play mostly Jimmy Reed-style rhythm and blues, which was lovely, sort of drunken, decadent stuff. Great.' At that time they knew Eric Clapton solely as one of the 'Kingston crowd', a bunch of kids in their late teens who used to go drinking at week-ends, although his attention to clothes set him apart from his scruffier companions.

Samwell-Smith played lead guitar in those days. One night, when they finished their set, Clapton emerged from the audience and asked him to make a promise; when he asked what, Clapton said never to play lead guitar again. Samwell-Smith took up bass.

By the time the Yardbirds were formed, Chris Dreja was playing rhythm guitar, Tony 'Top' Topham was lead guitarist and Jim McCarty, who had previously played in a Shadows-style school group with Samwell-Smith, was drummer. McCarty's introduction to rhythm and blues was typical of the time. 'The first time I heard R&B was through Paul,' he recalls. 'I went round to his house and he said, "I've got to play you this, it's *Jimmy Reed At Carnegie Hall* – it's this rhythm and blues stuff." I thought it was fantastic and we started to get a bit more. Then we went and saw the Stones and there was something happening, it was quite exciting actually. They'd started at the Crawdaddy Club, and we used to go there every week and watch them. It was a whole new thing.'

Although the group conscientiously avoided duplicating Stones numbers, comparisons were inevitable – and not merely because of Keith Relf's long hair, harmonica and maracas à la Mick Jagger. McCarty admits that their early sources of material were extremely limited: 'There were only really about two Chuck Berry albums, that Jimmy Reed one, a Howlin' Wolf album – *Moanin' In The Moonlight* [which included the classic "Smokestack Lightnin' "] – and a Slim Harpo one. And that was about it. Then we made some up just to get the time through, because we were playing three-hour sets, and an occasional slow one. It was all twelve-bar things. On our first few gigs every single number was twelve bars, but then we broke away from that, because they got a bit boring after a while.'

Far from harming the group's chances, initially at least, comparison with the Stones brought the Yardbirds the best seats on the substitutes' bench as the Stones began pulling out of their club residencies. The Stones' tour with the Everly Brothers, which also included Bo Diddley and was, according to one *Melody Maker* reader, less than perfectly billed, since, 'many R&B fans left the theatre after the Rolling Stones and Diddley appeared, and those who stayed chanted for the reappearance of Bo and the Stones – much to the annoyance of the Everly fans,' kept them on the road throughout October.

At the Crawdaddy Club Giorgio Gomelsky asked the Yardbirds to deputize. The Stones' loyal followers, indignant at their heroes' departure, at first resented the arrival of these newcomers and there was unrest within the group itself. Topham, according to Jim McCarty, 'was a bit too young and he wasn't really good enough'. Samwell-Smith puts it differently: 'He wasn't bad, he was very strange. He was into his own kind of blues, which didn't seem to be derivative of anything that any of us liked very much. He was good in his way, very good, but just strange. He certainly didn't fit in with what we wanted to play.' Whatever the precise reasons, he was asked to leave and Keith Relf invited Eric Clapton to join. A year and a half later, with the bitterness of hindsight, Clapton informed a *Melody Maker* reporter, 'I'd heard this group were interested in me joining them. I went to the Crawdaddy, walked in and thought, "What is this?" They were playing things like "Can't Judge A Book", sort of everyday R&B. Like R&B puppets. I don't know why but I thought what a cushy job this would be so I joined them.'

Clapton made an immediate contribution to the group's music. Samwell-Smith recalls, 'He could pick things up very quickly, and he was very keen on B. B. King – he used to worship B. B. King – and actually knew a lot about the blues, he really did know his music. He'd only got to hear a thing once and he'd be influenced by it, he could pick it up. He was an amazing guitarist, he was certainly the most lyrical guitarist I've ever known.' Nor, according to Samwell-Smith, did he contribute solely in his role as guitarist. 'I was all for going along with the rough and ready R&B stuff, the Jimmy Reed, John Lee Hooker – sort of very rough, drunken blues was my thing – and Eric was bringing in influences at that time of contemporary pop R&B [like the Vibrations' "My Girl Sloopy"] that was going on in America. He was always introducing new ideas, which was very good.'

Within a matter of weeks the 'most blueswailing' Yardbirds, as Gomelsky promoted them, won over the Crawdaddy's Sunday night crowd. Soon they were appearing regularly at another Gomelsky venue, the Star in Croydon's London Road on Saturday evenings, had taken over the Stones' residency at Ken Colyer's club in Great Newport Street, W.C.2., and were working the Ricky Tick club circuit. Early in 1964 they made it into the Marquee Club, which, abandoning its earlier antagonism to all but the most 'authentic' rhythm and blues, was featuring R&B groups with increasing frequency.

During this period the group first played with the American bluesman Sonny Boy Williamson. Williamson had come over to Britain in October 1963 as part of a blues package show which included Muddy Waters, Otis Spann, Lonnie Johnson, Memphis Slim and Willie Dixon. The 'American Negro Blues Festival' was held at the Fairfield Hall, Croydon, on 18 October, and Sonny

Boy Williamson ridiculing the know-alls' niggling objections
that he was in fact only Sonny Boy Williamson *II*, otherwise
known as Alex 'Rice' Miller, went down a storm with the large
and enthusiastic audience. He stayed on for six months and
toured the R&B clubs, where his virtuoso harmonica-playing
and showmanship – he took to sporting a two-tone city suit,
bowler hat, rolled umbrella and briefcase, in which he carried his
harmonicas and a bottle of whisky – earned him a unique and
legendary reputation among those bluesmen that visited
Britain.

On his many club appearances he was backed by a variety of
British R&B groups: the Animals, Cyril Davies' All-Stars,
Georgie Fame and the Blue Flames, Gary Farr and the T-Bones,
and the Yardbirds, of whom Sonny Boy is reputed to have said,
'Those boys play so sweet they wanna make me cry.' Certainly he
remarked of British R&B groups in general, 'I enjoy hearing
them singing blues here; it makes me feel good. In the States you
don't have no white boys sing the blues.'

The Yardbirds backed him at the Crawdaddy Club, where a
live session in front of a members-only Sunday night audience on
8 December was recorded, although it was more than two years
before the *Sonny Boy Williamson With The Yardbirds* album
appeared; they played with him at the Marquee at the start of
their residency there in January 1964; and they did a short tour
for Ricky Tick club promoter Philip Hayward a month later.
Hayward remembers, 'Sonny Boy Williamson was the biggest
ever. We ended up booking him for a fortnight every night. And
we put him in Windsor, Guildford, Maidenhead, Reading, Wat-
ford, Bath, Farnborough – anywhere we could get a hall, because
I had him for twenty quid a night. At Maidenhead [Pearce Hall]
we had a thousand and eighty people. I paid the Yardbirds
fifteen pounds and Sonny Boy twenty. I always remember we
were going to charge six shillings, which in those days was a few
bob, and we opened the door and they were ten deep, and my
partner said, "Christ, what shall we do?" I said, "I think we ought
to put it up to seven and six."' The recorded Crawdaddy Club
session captured much of the atmosphere of their performances
together and provided occasional glimpses of the rapidly growing talent of Eric Clapton.

By this time the Rolling Stones had elevated British rhythm
and blues from the grassroots club circuit into the top ten when
their second single, Lennon and McCartney's made-to-measure
R&B pastiche, 'I Wanna Be Your Man', reached No. 10 in the first
week of January. When their third single, a Bo Diddley-
influenced remake of Buddy Holly's 'Not Fade Away', made

third place in the charts in March the scrawl was on the wall in letters ten feet high. The music industry read the message and understood. The R&B boom had truly begun. Even the most successful trad acts were affected, although Kenny Ball insisted in *Record Mirror*, 'I don't think there is an R&B boom, but there most definitely is a boom in a form of music that people like to attach the tag "Rhythm and Blues" to. Consequently all the beat and rock groups who can get a member to play harmonica after a fashion are calling themselves R&B groups.'

Before 'Come On' the only British R&B records were Blues Incorporated's budget-priced album *R&B From The Marquee* and Cyril Davies' single, 'Country Line Special'; in the second half of 1963, following the release of 'Come On', a few more singles appeared: Cyril Davies' 'Preachin' the Blues', Manfred Mann's 'Why Should We Not?' and 'Cock-A-Hoop', the Paramounts' 'Poison Ivy', and the Blue Flames' 'Orange Street'. But the Stones' success opened the floodgates. Between March and May debut singles were released by no less than five major R&B groups: the Animals' 'Baby Let Me Take You Home', the Graham Bond Organization's 'Long Tall Shorty', the Pretty Things' 'Rosalyn', the Spencer Davis Group's 'Dimples', and the Yardbirds' 'I Wish You Would'.

Under the guidance of Giorgio Gomelsky, who by then was managing the group, the Yardbirds had done a demo session at R. G. Jones' studio in Morden. The recording was supervised by Mike Vernon, then a staff producer at Decca, who says, 'I think we only did two tracks – we might have done three, but only two of them ever saw the light of day. They were nothing spectacular, but at the time they were the epitome of what the Yardbirds were, they were exactly what the Yardbirds were all about. One of them was the Jimmy Reed song, "Baby What's Wrong?", and the other was a thing called "Honey In Your Hips", which was a song that the band wrote themselves, basically a Jimmy Reed/Billy Boy Arnold type of tune – in other words it was Chicago. That was what the Yardbirds were all about, because their influences were Jimmy Reed, Bo Diddley, Chuck Berry, Muddy Waters, B. B. King, they were the artists that they were drawing their material from in those days.

'[The demo] was done for Giorgio so that he could place the act with a record company, and he took it to Decca because of the involvement that I had with Decca, albeit it wasn't a particularly strong one at the time because the only act that I had with them that was making any kind of noise really was the Artwoods, who had been fairly successful in Germany. So when we'd made the demo, Giorgio brought it to Decca to Dick Rowe, who was then

the head of the pop A&R department, and I think really the
problem was that nobody at Decca understood it. I don't really
know whether anybody at any record company would have
understood it, quite honestly, because I don't think most record
companies understood the Rolling Stones either. It was something that was completely alien to them. Musically it was
something that nobody in this country in the record industry
had any experience with. For what reason should they have had?
No reason at all. In the case of the Rolling Stones, it was only
through a certain commitment in terms of *having* to like the
group and *having* to think that they were going to mean
something on the part of Noel Walker, that the Stones were
signed to Decca. And unfortunately the same kind of commitment wasn't forthcoming with the Yardbirds.'

Gomelsky took the demo to EMI, whose A&R staff were
anxiously searching for an answer to the Rolling Stones, and
secured a contract for the group on the Columbia label. And it
was Gomelsky who produced 'I Wish You Would' and 'A Certain
Girl' at Olympic studios around the end of March, the same
month a Marquee Club session was recorded for later release as
Five Live Yardbirds. Success was expected soon.

In April Hamish Grimes told *Melody Maker*, 'They are working
seven nights a week at very high prices. They are booked almost
solid for the next three months – and that is without a record.'
Since playing on the opening night at the Marquee's new premises at 90 Wardour Street, W.1., the group had appeared there
regularly every Friday. The club's manager, John Gee, tipped
them for stardom, saying 'The Yardbirds have got what the kids
seem to want.' Norman Jopling, 'investigating' British R&B in
Jazzbeat, wrote, 'They comprise one of the best groups musically, with that certain something that makes them different
from the average beat team. They're visually and audibly exciting and although they haven't yet broken through recordwise,
the odds are that in a few weeks they will have done.' In the same
issue the release of 'I Wish You Would' was announced, to which
news was added: 'All those who have heard the "test" pressing
have tipped it for the Top Twenty. The blueswailing five also
recorded for Granada TV in late April a programme starring the
famous folk group, Peter, Paul and Mary. 1964 is for all "mody-
bodys" the Yardbirds' Year!' And, as if to emphasize the imminent realization of these predictions, an R&B poll in *Record
Mirror* placed the group third among British bands behind the
Rolling Stones and Manfred Mann. The record was released on 1
May, but sold modestly. The Yardbirds stayed in the clubs.

During the summer they played a number of festivals, including the 4th National Jazz and Blues Festival, held at Richmond, and planned a second assault on the charts. Early in August pop journalist Chris Roberts reported on a Yardbirds gig in Kenton, Middlesex. 'They were loud ("the acoustics of the hall," said rhythm guitarist Chris Dreja), driving and powerful (drummer Jim McCarty broke a bass drum skin), and the vocals from singer-harmonica player Keith Relf were almost indistinguishable from the roar of the group – though at times he appeared to be trying to swallow the microphone.

'Lead guitarist Eric Clapton was very good, bass-guitarist Paul Samwell-Smith, the only one of the five to have had musical training, less so.

'Sonny Boy Williamson was right when he said British blues groups need to "cool it" to achieve a good blues sound.

'Volume doesn't heighten excitement – when it reaches the threshold of pain, you forget about the number and run away looking for a soundproof room and a record of "Whispering".

'Truthfully, the Yardbirds did have to contend with bad acoustics, and none of the audience seemed to be running away, but many people would still appreciate a "cooler" sound, especially on the quieter numbers.

'Criticism over. The group's overall instrumental sound, including Keith Relf's excellent harmonica, gives them a deserved spot on the R&B map. Their treatment of numbers, timing and endings were worth hearing for their professionalism.

'"We try to vary the styles of numbers – tempo and so on," said Eric in the nearby pub, where they drink with a few interruptions from young fans....

'"What would we call ourselves? Well, a sort of R&B group, I suppose, when you come down to it," said Eric.'

The Yardbirds' performance that night (like Roberts' report) was not untypical. The group did play loudly, though only by contemporary standards, and the musicianship, with the exception of Clapton's guitar work, was not outstanding. Moreover, Relf had problems with his voice. If he overburdened it, as he frequently did during long sets, it would disappear completely and he would often be unable to return after the interval until he had coaxed it back with tea taken with lemon and honey. On August Bank Holiday he collapsed and was subsequently taken to hospital for treatment of a punctured lung. The Authentics' Mick O'Neill deputized for him so that the group could play a few gigs, but the next single, which was due to be released on 4 September, was postponed. However, in September they were encouraged by the results of *MM*'s pop poll, which named them third Brightest Hope (behind Lulu and Zoot Money), and by

Relf's return later the same month.

Unfortunately, 'Good Morning Little Schoolgirl', when it was released late in October, did no better than its predecessor. Disc jockey Jimmy Savile felt it had 'a good beat for my clubs and dance halls and could enjoy a modicum of success', but he was being kind rather than realistic. The group wasn't happy with it, at least, according to Relf at the time, 'not as happy as we should be. I'm sure if we could go into the studio and do the same number again it would come out much better. We recorded it months ago, just before I was ill.' It seems unlikely that the group derived much consolation from the fact that another version of the same number, released shortly afterwards, sold in even fewer numbers. This was Rod Stewart's first solo recording.

In truth, what distinguished the Yardbirds' performances and was missing from their records, apart from brief moments as on the flipside, 'I Ain't Got You', of 'Good Morning Little School-girl', was the playing of Eric Clapton. His aggression was start-ling, and it was this feature of his playing (rather than his speed) that earned him his nickname, 'Slowhand', for he broke strings constantly and would restring his guitar to the accompaniment of a slow handclap led by the rest of the group and taken up in ritual by the crowd. If a gaggle of girls would always cluster around Keith Relf's microphone, the crowd at Clapton's feet was invariably larger, listened harder, and made more noise when he finished playing. 'It wasn't any kind of mass hysteria,' says Paul Samwell-Smith, 'because the masses didn't really know about him then. It was an in thing. Of the people who came to see the Yardbirds, some minority groups had sprung up, but certainly the largest minority group was that watching Eric. His side of the stage was always the one with the bunch of people just watching every move he made.'

Even without his guitar strapped on Clapton stood apart from the other Yardbirds. The rest dressed in a way that made them indistinguishable from countless groups on countless stages in clubs from London to Liverpool, but Eric, to the educated eye, was the embodiment of mod. His hair was neatly short, his clothes casual but correct in the kind of detail that distinguished the faces from the fakers. 'We just wore what we wore in the day,' he recalls, 'and I was living in London and actually came into contact with some very heavy mods. I used to spend all night walking round the West End looking in shoe shops.' But before mod was marketed in high street boutiques, it was shared only by an elite – a group so exclusive they didn't take to their style being paraded on stage, as Clapton had already discovered.

'When I started playing with the Roosters, I was in the first throes of being a mod and the little clique I was hanging out with down the Scene club – when we played there at the Scene they didn't like it, they didn't like me being a member of a group and wearing *our* uniform in this group, and they jeered at me and told me to piss off, and it was very difficult to ever become friends with them after that, because I'd broken their little circle and taken it into the public.'

As a guitarist he quickly advanced beyond the role of blues copyist towards an individuality without precedent among British guitarists. As a blues enthusiast who knew of Clapton's deep interest in the blues and shared his heroes, Mike Vernon knew better than most observers just how good a guitarist he was. 'He was great. There was a certain rawness about his playing in those days which I suppose can't be captured again. It's very hard to capture that kind of thing. There were other guitar players around, but he somehow had managed to latch onto the same kind of fire and attack and the same kind of flowing phrase that B. B. King and Freddie King were so good at doing. He was the only guitarist at the time who actually latched onto it and was able to relate to it and reproduce it. That was where he scored: that he was able to reproduce it. There might have been plenty of other guitarists around who thought that they were able to do it, but they weren't making it. And, of course, there were subsequently other guitarists who came along, because he put it on the map as far as this country was concerned – and it *was* a distinctive style of guitar playing, inasmuch as so is Django Rheinhart's style of guitar playing unique, so is Joe Pass', so is Wes Montgomery's. And there are the guitarists within the rock field who have created their own style that people have moulded themselves on. And Eric did that, although the inspiration came from Freddie King and B. B. King and Magic Sam and Otis Rush, from those records. That was sufficient inspiration for him.

'Eric could play Chuck Berry licks, Jimmy Reed licks, T-Bone Walker licks, which is no great shakes, but he had all those off pat. He could play all that stuff because he was into blues. But there were probably lots of other guitar players around at the time who were also into Freddie King and B. B. King, but who didn't have the technical ability to be able to translate it. And Eric had it. Eric was the one, there wasn't anybody else. There were plenty of other guitar players around – there was Roger Dean with John Mayall, Bernie Watson – but they were all playing the same thing, they were all playing Chuck Berry and they were all playing those T-Bone Walker type of licks. There was nobody who could get out there and play that Freddie King type of stuff except Eric. He was the only one.'

The brilliance of their lead guitarist offered scant compensation for the unfulfilled ambitions of the Yardbirds. The euphoria of the early summer had given way to a wintry discontent. Little happened in the late months of 1964 that followed Keith Relf's recovery apart from a tour with Billy J. Kramer and the promise of a spot on the Beatles' Christmas show, due to open at Hammersmith Odeon on Christmas Eve. Worse still, waiting on the brink of the yawning chasm that separated the clubs from the charts for the slightest twitch of a beckoning gesture from the other side was an uncomfortable position. Already they could feel the chill breeze of resentment at their back as their fans sensed their eagerness to depart. Clapton declared at the time, 'Club audiences are very possessive, and when records start selling the kids come up to you and say, "We've lost you". We had that feeling at the Crawdaddy. Then we left for a while to do a tour with Billy J. Kramer. When we played the Crawdaddy last Sunday it wasn't quite the same again.'

What kept them flat-footed on the edge for so long in flagrant contradiction of the universal prophecies of stardom was, according to Samwell-Smith, the fact that they were standing in the shadow of the Stones. 'They started before us, they went into the Crawdaddy Club in Richmond before us, they left that and started out on the road. We did all the same things, but always three to six months behind the Rolling Stones, and so we never had a chance. We were always being compared, and the Rolling Stones were breaking the ground as far as long hair and bad behaviour went.'

It was at the time of the Beatles' Christmas show, where they were warmly, if not ecstatically, received by the impatient fans of the Fab Four, that they were approached by their music publishers, Feldman's, with a song called 'For Your Love'. It was like nothing the Yardbirds had done before and Giorgio Gomelsky didn't much like it. Paul Samwell-Smith, however, had been pestering him for an opportunity to produce a record and, having had no luck himself, Gomelsky was content to relinquish the task to the bass guitarist. The song had originally been written for Manchester's Mockingbirds by guitarist Graham Gouldman (later a member of 10cc along with fellow Mockingbird Kevin Godley), but their recording of it had already been rejected by their record company, who evidently had less imagination than Samwell-Smith. He had long wanted to use a harpsichord on record and felt that 'For Your Love' provided the perfect setting. The record, essentially, was his – not the Yardbirds'. 'It wasn't,' he says, 'an agreed policy. It was like I said, "Oh, let me produce this one," and everyone said, "All right, let's see what happens, it can't do any harm." It wasn't anything to do with R&B at all. It was about two and a half minutes long, and only fifteen seconds in the middle was the Yardbirds playing anything like the Yardbirds. The rest of it was session guys playing harpsichord and bass and bongos and just Keith Relf, Jim McCarty and I singing. It had virtually nothing to do with the Yardbirds and certainly nothing to do with rhythm and blues.'

Reviewing 'For Your Love' in the first week of March 1965, the *Melody Maker*'s Ray Coleman described the record as 'their most commercial so far. The group that has hovered on the brink of stardom for so long ought to hit big with this one. It goes, and the arrangement is good.' A week later the paper reported: 'Eric Clapton, lead guitarist with the Yardbirds, has left the group because, he says, "They are going too commercial." '

Keith Relf, who announced Clapton's replacement by Jeff Beck of the Tridents, explained, 'It's very sad because we are all friends. There were no bad feelings at all, but Eric did not get on well at all with the business. He does not like commercialization. He loves the blues so much I suppose he did not like it being played badly by a white shower like us! Eric did not like our new record, "For Your Love". He should have been featured, but he did not want to sing or anything and he only did that boogie bit in the middle. His leaving is bound to be a blow to the group's image at first, because Eric was very popular. Jeff Beck, who is very, very good, was recommended to us by session man Jimmy Page, who is the guv'nor.'

The following week 'For Your Love' was the highest entry in the top fifty at No. 34. Within a fortnight the group had appeared twice on BBC Television's *Top Of The Pops* and the record stood at No. 4 in the charts.

Under such circumstances Clapton's departure took on an air of quite extraordinary idealism, which was only retrospectively illuminated by conduct later in his career. It was one thing to condemn other groups for 'going commercial', quite another to kick the ladder away the moment the first rung was within reach. Less than six months earlier he had expressed indignation at 'the snobs who say they don't like an artist any more because he has a hit record. Why is it criminal to be successful?'

Yet he was not turning his back on success *per se*, but rather on its concomitants, as Paul Samwell-Smith subsequently realized. 'I don't know if Eric wanted success then, certainly not that kind of success where it meant standing on stage repeating the same old hit songs – pop top twenty songs – note for note every time, that you hadn't written, that you didn't like. That's

how he saw it, I'm sure. I produced the record and got some fun
out of it, but every time I played it on stage I just got bored with
it. We started evolving a policy of the group around one side
incident that happened a few months earlier, which was me
producing the record. And it's the wrong way to go about things.
The product takes over the group – I think Eric was right. It was
worse for him because he didn't even produce it and didn't get
any fun out of it; he certainly didn't get any money out of it. I
don't blame him for leaving at all. I wish I'd left then.' Samwell-
Smith quit just over a year later in June 1966.

Although Graham Gouldman will admit with a grin that his
song was the cause of Clapton's quitting, 'For Your Love' was
undoubtedly a mere catalyst for Clapton's feelings about the
group. Samwell-Smith admits that the Yardbirds were 'a messy
institution anyway. We were working too hard, too many nights
a week, not enough time off to even rehearse, we were living in
each other's pockets all the time. We weren't very nice to each
other.' The responsibility for overworking the group was Giorgio
Gomelsky's: although inventive, inspired at times, his ambitions
for the group ignored the musicians' own inclinations. Perhaps
the truest estimate of the situation was Clapton's own,
expressed a year later: 'Eventually I got brainwashed with this
commercial R&B, brainwashed most of the time – it was only
when I got on stage away from all the hubble bubble, that I
realized I didn't really like what the group did or played.
Anyway, the whole thing got so businesslike with finances,
companies, promotion and all that, we became machines instead
of human beings. I thought, "If I'm going to become a money-
making musical factory, I'll pull out", so I did.'

The effect on the group of Clapton's departure was far from
disastrous. 'For Your Love' went on to reach No. 2, and the
change of fortune that accompanied the Yardbirds' change of
style was too good to ignore. Keith Relf said as much to *Record
Mirror*: 'Rhythm and blues is becoming what trad became and
we're going to change some of our numbers. We're getting away
from the old twelve-bar bit and doing other things.' The new
approach brought them four more top ten hits in twelve months
(two tailor-made by Gouldman after hearing Jeff Beck play with
them and two by members of the group) and also broke them in
the States, where Beck and Jimmy Page, who joined the line-up
a year later, established a following that guaranteed subsequent
success for the Jeff Beck Group and, especially, Led Zeppelin.

Meanwhile, Clapton took off to Oxford, where Ben Palmer was
living, and asked if he would put him up in his flat. During
Clapton's time with the Yardbirds they had met only once,

briefly, at the Beatles' Christmas show, for Palmer, who had 'the puritanical view of someone who was still convinced that Otis Spann was the last thing that would ever happen,' took small interest in the career of the Yardbirds. Clapton stayed a while, reading a lot, playing guitar a little, talking less about his plans. He visited the Ashmolean museum and looked at pictures. Then John Mayall phoned to ask if he would join the Bluesbreakers. Clapton was initially hesitant, reluctant to commit himself once more to a band so soon after leaving the Yardbirds. Eventually he rang Mayall and told him he was returning to London. He would join the Bluesbreakers.

Three

JOHN MAYALL'S BLUESBREAKERS – RAMBLIN' ON MY MIND

John Mayall always was an eccentric. Even in a world where normal people were nonconformist he stood out as an extraordinary figure. Ricky Tick promoter Philip Hayward remembers a phone call from Alexis Korner in the club's early days that went like this: 'Philip, I've got a friend coming down from Manchester. He's a nice fellow, he makes his own musical instruments. They call him John Mayall. He's a strange bloke, he lives up a tree and drinks vegetable juices, but give him twenty quid and he'll come down.' Improbable, but barely exaggerated.

Born in 1933, Mayall was one of the pioneers of British blues. After National Service, he led his first group at art college, eventually teaming up with a semi-professional jazz drummer, Hughie Flint, to form Blues Syndicate. Flint recalls, 'There was John on electric piano, harmonica and guitar, me on drums, then there was a rhythm guitarist with a transistor radio for an amplifier, an alto saxophone player and a trumpet player – there was no bass. And we just played endless riffs and John sang songs that he'd heard and this and that.'

Considerably encouraged by Alexis Korner, whose appearances with Blues Incorporated at Manchester's Bodega Jazz Club allowed him the chance to seek advice and to sit in with accomplished musicians, Mayall took his band to London in 1963 to play a couple of gigs, at the Ricky Tick club and at Alexis Korner's Blues City, located at the Empire Rooms, Tottenham Court Road, W.1., where he was billed as 'London's newest raving R&B sensation, the "Roland Kirk" of the R&B world playing three instruments'. Further encouraged by Korner and the southern audiences' reception of his music, Mayall moved to London later in the year, found a job as a graphic designer, and set about forming a new band.

According to Flint, who followed him south later, the Bluesbreakers' first guitarist, Bernie Watson, formerly with Cyril Davies' All-Stars, was 'a phenomenal guitarist. I think he was basically a classical guitarist, but he'd learned to play blues. He used to sit with his back to the audience. Then Bernie left and there was a series of guitarists. I can't remember their names because there were three guitarists in a row all in the space of about a month. This was where John learned to hire and fire people. Eventually he found Roger Dean, who was a very good guitarist, but mainly from the country style – Chet Atkins and that stuff – a very good guitarist, but not quite suited to John's style of blues. I don't know how John found John McVie, but he was there when I arrived. He lived in Ealing – very young, and a very solid bass player. Nothing adventurous, but very solid. Roger Dean stayed with the band about a year, until Eric joined, doing all the up-and-down-the-country gigs for thirty and forty pounds and sleeping in Salvation Army hostels.'

Mayall recorded one single, 'Crawling Up A Hill'/'Mr James' with Bernie Watson, John McVie, and another drummer (probably Peter Ward) shortly before Flint joined, and then cut a live album at Klooks Kleek – a linchpin of the London R&B club circuit, located in the Railway Hotel, West Hampstead – with Roger Dean, McVie and Flint. 'It was,' says Flint, 'a very bright, interesting album. It was indicative of what John was doing at the time – very rough and ready blues. His songs in those days were quite naïve and had very simple lyrics, but he used to do other people's songs as well occasionally, which were quite good.' And there was another single, 'Crocodile Walk'/'Blues City Shakedown', Mayall's last recording with that line-up. It was also his last recording with Decca for a while.

Shortly before the release of 'Crocodile Walk' in April 1965, Mayall learned of Clapton's departure from the Yardbirds and resolved to have him in the band. This decision was apparently based on hearing one short Clapton solo on a Yardbirds record: most likely 'I Ain't Got You', the B-side of 'Good Morning Little Schoolgirl', where in a few brief moments he played Superman to the group's Clark Kent. 'We were playing some gig in Nottingham,' says Flint, 'and he gathered us round this little record player and said to me and John McVie, "Listen to this guitar player and tell me what you think." So we listened to it and said, "Yes, that sounds very good, John." He said, "Well, that's Eric Clapton, and he's just left the Yardbirds, so shall we ask him to join?" So we said, "Yeah." But Eric was very dubious about actually joining. John said, "Well, look, we're playing blues, you're a blues guitarist, you've got nothing to lose." Eventually he persuaded him to join. There were no rehearsals: I met him in the street, we got in the van and went off to the first gig, wherever it was, and Eric just played like only Eric can play. He must have heard of John, he'd obviously heard of the band, because we had been working for over a year in London. I think he was just a bit dubious about joining another band straightaway after the Yardbirds.' Left in the cold, Roger Dean rejoined his old group, the Newnotes.

For Clapton, one of the attractions of the Bluesbreakers was Mayall's strong leadership, the antithesis of the Yardbirds' haphazard mismanagement, as well as his unswerving commitment to the music he wanted to play. Yet within a matter of months that attraction had grown too weak to ward off a bout of wanderlust. In August he announced his intention to leave the Bluesbreakers for a world tour with a bunch of amateur musicians. If he was enjoying playing with the Bluesbreakers, life off stage must have been less congenial. Since he had no money when he joined the band, it was arranged that he should stay *en famille* with Mayall, so all he generally saw during a hectic period of work was the inside of tiny dressing rooms, the inside of the Bluesbreakers' van and the inside of Mayall's house.

Besides, the tour was an inviting prospect, an adventure which promised, as much as music, the company of a number of people he liked and admired.

The tour was the brainchild of Ted Milton. It was his inspiration and enthusiasm that convinced a quite disparate group that attempting to play their way round the world would be an enjoyable and rewarding way to spend an indefinite amount of time. The party that set off for Greece, their first intended destination, comprised Clapton, Ben Palmer, John Bailey as singer, Bernie Greenwood, who was a doctor and had played saxophone with Chris Farlowe, Bob Ray, an ex-trad trumpet player who learned to play bass guitar en route, and Ted's brother Jake, who later joined Quintessence, as drummer. They called themselves the Glands.

Unfortunately it took them so long to reach Athens that on their arrival it was time for Jake Milton to return to England, and they were obliged to look for a local replacement. One was found by the club which hired them. 'As far as I remember,' says Palmer, 'he was a pilot. He'd often come in an hour or two late because there was cloud over Cyprus or some other unlikely reason. He didn't speak any English and we didn't speak any Greek, but he seemed to enjoy himself.'

This first engagement was also the Glands' last. According to Palmer, 'We played in the most unsuitable possible place, which was a ritzy night-club. We played from about eight or nine in the evening until it shut, which was sometimes eight or nine in the morning. We'd never rehearsed or ever played together – any of us, except Eric and I had played together years before – and we had no common musical background at all. And the demands of the night-club owner were pretty stringent. What he wanted was to bill us as a band from Liverpool, and that we should play what was slowly filtering through into Greece as being the latest in English pop music. So we got to playing early Stones numbers, early Kinks numbers; we stuck in a few of our own, hoping they wouldn't be noticeably too different from the rest of the repertoire; we did some Ray Charles. And we never satisfied them.

'We were quite unsuitable for the club, and the club was quite unsuitable for us, and we were only the second band anyway. We were only doing the dog's work: the stars were the local Greek band. It was a summer season place only. It was very expensive. We hadn't bothered with work permits at all, and we hadn't bothered with import licences for all the equipment and the instruments. We hated the food, and that wasn't just the normal run of musicians' obsession with chips and all things fried or macrobiotics, it was simply that Greek food is bloody awful. That upset us, the management never paid us, and right in the middle of us trying to get out of this dreadful situation – because we were desperately miserable by then – the other band, the main band, had a big motor accident, a very serious one, most of them were killed and the rest weren't able to work again, and that left us having to hold the whole thing together: still not getting paid, very bolshy and very miserable, past the point of being able to laugh about it.

'It's a long and complicated story, but we did end up in a very dicey situation indeed. We didn't have the money to leave the country, we were working illegally because they were paying the police off; they weren't paying us at all, they treated us abominably, and as the first Yardbirds records had just come into Greece they realized what they'd got their hands on in Eric and he was virtually a captive. When he did finally leave the country, it was almost like a James Bond novel, hiding in toilets at the station, and abandoning his clothes and a very good early Marshall amplifier. We just left it – anything to be able to get out.'

On his return, Clapton wasted no time in contacting John Mayall. Hughie Flint recalls, 'I think Eric just rang John up and said, "Hello, I'm back," and John said, "Oh right, well, d'you want your job back?" So the unfortunate guy (Jeff Kribbett of Dr K's Blues Band) who'd been playing guitar at that point was given the golden elbow, and Eric came back in.'

It was during this second phase with the Bluesbreakers that

Clapton really made a name for himself (and for John Mayall's Bluesbreakers as a whole), single-handedly elevating the status of group guitarist to popular hero – the 'Eric is God' idolatry dates from this time – laying the foundation for a second British blues boom, which would throw up countless Clapton imitators over the next few years. 'When he came back,' says Flint, 'things went from strength to strength. It was like the Eric Clapton show, it wasn't John Mayall's Bluesbreakers – there were more people coming along to see Eric. He was an incredible draw in the band. He got better and better. It was like hearing Charlie Parker with Jay McShann. You know that there's this genius there hidden among this morass of rather naïve sound. He knocked me out from the start, because he was playing blues like I'd only heard negroes play prior to that.'

During Clapton's absence a significant change had occurred within the Bluesbreakers. John McVie had departed in October and Mayall brought in Jack Bruce, who had recently left the Graham Bond Organization. According to Flint, his arrival prompted the band's only rehearsal. 'And I think that was because Jack insisted. John's way of introducing new songs was singing them in the van going to gigs. And it would be a very loose format. It was a similar format for most songs: it would be an intro, then he'd sing a couple of choruses, then there'd be a couple of choruses on guitar, then a couple more choruses vocal, then out. He'd occasionally arrange things in a little more detail, but most of it was fairly rough and ready. [With Jack] things *really* started to get improvised. Solos would be chorus after chorus after chorus, whereas before it was just the usual two choruses solo. Jack was obviously a big stimulus to Eric.' In December Bruce was seduced by the prospect of bigger audiences and higher wages into joining Manfred Mann, prompting Mayall to write 'Double Crossing Time' and to rehire John McVie.

However, during those few weeks he had made an indelible impression on Clapton. Asked soon after to name his favourite artists, Eric replied, 'Some artists I have worked with are not widely known as being great and are to many people obscure. Jack Bruce is definitely one of them. He's the best bass player I know.' He also said, 'I intend to stay with John Mayall unless I get the chance to form my own group sometime.' These statements later proved to be not unconnected.

John Mayall and the Bluesbreakers had recorded two sides for Andrew Oldham's Immediate label during Clapton's first stint with the group. 'I'm Your Witchdoctor' and 'Telephone Blues', both Mayall compositions and produced by Jimmy Page, were released in October, shortly before Clapton's return. One reviewer wrote: 'Knockout uptempo number written by singer-organist Mayall. Hums along with some gas points of unison with a vocal and the blues guitar of Eric Clapton. A superb disc which deserves to be a hit.' But it wasn't. It was, however, distinguished by a sustained, disembodied wail from Clapton's ancient Gibson Les Paul, a bittersweet cry of pain and pleasure that was to characterize much of his work with Cream. The band did not record for Immediate again.

Shortly after his return from Greece, Clapton did some sessions for a Champion Jack Dupree album, *From New Orleans To Chicago*, which Mike Vernon was producing for Decca. Mayall also played on the sessions, along with the Groundhogs' guitarist Tony McPhee, and Malcolm Pool (bass) and Keef Hartley (drums) from the Artwoods. Vernon had set up his own independent record label to release specialist blues material which would not otherwise be readily available, and the growing popularity of blues in Britain had encouraged him to consider branching out to record his own material. 'To be able to do that,' he says, 'it was a necessity for us to have an act that we'd know we'd be able to sell. By then I'd got to know John, so I approached him and put the cards on the table. I said, "How about making a real downhome blues record with just the two of you, and we'll split the profits, and we'll have some fun." He'd already said to me he was thinking of going back to Decca, and said, "If I go back, would you be interested in producing me?" So, of course, I said yes. So we did it. We went to the old Wessex studios in Soho and we did it straight mono: one microphone stuck up in the middle of the studio, just piano, voice and a guitar, and to this day it's the only record I've ever made that sounds as if it was made in Chicago.

And it really does. I remember a lot of people when they reviewed it mentioning Eric's heavy-handed guitar playing on it, which I couldn't understand at all. To me that's one of the finest guitar efforts he's ever put on record – "Lonely Years" in particular, because it just epitomizes what Eric was about at that time. To him playing that kind of thing, like we were discussing at the time, it was like Big Boy Spires, who was a guitarist working out of Chicago, and also Robert Junior Lockwood, it was that kind of a *down* feel. And to this day to me it's still a great little record.' It was far less polished than Jimmy Page's production of 'I'm Your Witchdoctor' for Immediate, and the fact that Mayall chose Vernon to produce the album he subsequently recorded for Decca indicates which approach he himself favoured. As one reviewer asserted, it was 'an extraordinarily authentic sound', and the demand for such authenticity even exceeded Vernon's estimation, as his original pressing of five hundred copies on his Purdah label quickly sold out when the record was released early in August 1966.

Nobody was expecting a hit when John Mayall and the Blues-breakers went into Decca's West Hampstead studios to record their *Blues Breakers* album. The budget was small, they were allocated the No. 2 studio, which was undersized and ill-equipped, and the engineer assisting Vernon, Gus Dudgeon, was as inexperienced as the producer. To make matters worse, the musicians were unsympathetic to Vernon's problems. 'John didn't know what the hell was going on as far as technical terms were concerned,' he recalls, 'he was just interested in making the music. And Eric would play loud, which we hadn't had to contend with before, and Hughie was loud, but the snare wasn't as loud as anything else so we had a problem getting that, and John McVie would usually end up having a few too many drinks. So in one way or another there were lots of little hang-ups.'

Clapton, in fact, resolutely refused to follow the rules of the recording studio, setting his equipment up as he did at every gig and insisting his amp stayed *loud*. 'He had a terrible time with the engineer,' says Hughie Flint, 'because he wanted his amp up, which meant that it was distorting, and Gus Dudgeon was tearing his hair out, saying, "You turn down, we'll do it in here," and Eric said, "No, I can't play unless I play like I play on stage." The result's there for posterity, what he did – which countless other guitarists have done since – which is play with fuzz and the actual distortion that he used to play through his amplifier. No one else was doing it at the time, they were all playing clean notes. He was playing dirty. He was the most aggressive guitar player I'd heard. Ever.'

Apart from the force of his playing, *Blues Breakers* was notable for the inclusion of Clapton's first solo vocal on record. His own inhibitions had prevented him from ever singing on stage with the Bluesbreakers, and it took much persuasion and the right song, 'Ramblin' On My Mind' by his hero Robert Johnson, to make him sing in the studio. When he heard his voice back in the control box, he is reputed to have exclaimed, 'God, it's horrible, I hate it!' Yet it was an extremely convincing effort. While not entirely assured, his singing was unmannered and sincere; the whole performance of the number, recorded by Clapton and Mayall on their own, was close to the earlier Purdah recordings and to the spirit of Robert Johnson.

In spite of all the problems encountered in the studio – and, to some extent, *because* of them – the right atmosphere for record-

ing the band was established. 'Technically speaking,' Mike
Vernon admits, '*Blues Breakers* would never win any awards,
not for the best recorded album of all time, though it might win a
few for the worst recorded, but it was the music that counted, so
it didn't really matter. Any problems we had, we just shrugged
our shoulders and said, "Well, that's the blues," and we'd just get
on with it, because there was a certain lackadaisical manner,
there was a certain amount of an attitude that said, "Well, who
really cares? If the music sounds right and it feels good, then who
really cares if we've got a bit too much top here or if we're going
to have a bit of a curve problem when we cut the master, well,
that's somebody else's problem. Let's just make the music." So
we didn't concern ourselves too much with it. But I don't think
for fire and drive and for sheer energy that John bettered that
album at any time. At all. The energy that was created by the
band when Eric was with them was special. And we were lucky:
we captured it on that one record, and it's never been captured
since, and I don't ever imagine it will be again. It's just one of
those rare things that happen. The chemistry was right.'

The achievement of *Blues Breakers* was indeed in capturing
the spirit of the band in the recording studio. Considering the
musicians' own limited experience of recording, their playing is
remarkably unconstrained. Perhaps Clapton lost a little edge,
maybe as much as an everlasting blade after a single shave, but
that impression was encouraged by the lack of his physical
presence out front, eyes closed, head tilted slightly backwards,
those magical hands conjuring the most emotional of sounds
from his guitar. Essentially all that was missing from the live
performance were the cries of the Clapton contingent in the
crowd: the blues freaks, the guitar freaks, worshipping at his feet,
chanting 'We want more God!' and 'Give God a solo!'

The album was not without flaws. Mayall's two harmonica
features, 'Parchman Farm' and 'Another Man', suffered greatly
in transposition from the stage, where they were invariably
extended into bravura displays of virtuosity, to a few short,
sterile minutes in the studio, where there was no crowd to please;
'What'd I Say', likewise, with its obligatory drum solo was only
briefly brightened by Clapton's witty steal from the Beatles'
'Day Tripper'. The horns which augmented the Bluesbreakers'
line-up on several tracks were generally too precise, clearly
anxious not to intrude, altogether too polite.

Clapton's guitar work was of a different dimension. Whether on
his guitar showpieces like Freddie King's 'Hideaway' or 'Steppin' Out' or tearing the heart out of Mayall compositions like
'Have You Heard' or the Mayall/Clapton song 'Double Crossing

Time', the effect was physical. His Les Paul could make the skin crawl up the listener's spine till it bristled the hair at the back of the neck. If not deity, he was at least superman.

Mayall, unrenowned for self-effacement, took the unprecedented step of giving his guitarist individual billing on the album sleeve in letters almost as tall as those that spelled his own name. Thus: JOHN MAYALL WITH ERIC CLAPTON. If he resented being upstaged by Clapton, he certainly never showed it. After all, why should he? The band's name had become firmly established since Clapton joined in April 1965; his success was Mayall's.

Clapton, however, was not content. Interviewed in a mood of despondency in March 1966, he said, 'I don't think there will be room for me here much longer. None of my music is English – it is rooted in Chicago. I represent what is going on in Chicago at the moment, the best I can anyway, because it's difficult to get all the records imported.... Anyway I think the only way is to go to America. Forming a blues band in England is like banging your head against a brick wall. Nobody wants to do it, and nobody wants to record it. I'm not interested in guitar, sound, technique, but in people and what you can do to them via music. I'm very conceited and I think I have a power – and my guitar is a medium for expressing that power. I don't need people to tell me how good I am, I've worked it out by myself. It's nothing to do with technique, and rehearsing, it's to do with the person behind that guitar who is trying to find an outlet. My guitar is a medium through which I can make contact to myself. It's very, very lonely. This is blues. Expression. I am contacting myself through the guitar and telling myself I have a power. I haven't a girlfriend or any other relationship so I tell myself of this power through the guitar.' Evidently public adulation was convincing him that he genuinely did possess extraordinary powers beyond his ability as a guitarist, while on the other hand he felt oppressed by the phlegmatism of the record industry. Or perhaps it was merely his recurring restlessness that brought him down.

In contrast the band was at a peak. According to a report of a gig in June, 'For the third time in as many months, John Mayall's Bluesbreakers brought the house down at London's Marquee Club, last Thursday. During the wailing first half the audience would have been swinging on the rafters had there been any. Eric Clapton on guitar played like a maestro, weaving, bending, attacking and soaring his way through a programme of blues classics ... Mayall leaped and soloed on a hectic version of "Parchman Farm", while Clapton was highlighted on such numbers as "Stormy Monday", "So Many Roads", and the fiery

Freddie King instrumental "Hideaway".'

That Marquee gig was one of Clapton's last with Mayall's band. In July 1966 he quit to form Cream with Jack Bruce and Ginger Baker. Precisely when the idea of the trio was first formed is not known, although the first approach to Clapton was made by Baker at a Bluesbreakers gig in Oxford, but what is clear is that Bruce, Baker and Clapton had been rehearsing for some time before Mayall discovered the truth. Like a lot of other people, he read the news in *Melody Maker* in June: 'A sensational new "Groups' Group" starring Eric Clapton, Jack Bruce and Ginger Baker is being formed.... The group say they hope to start playing at clubs, ballrooms and theatres in a month's time. It is expected they will remain as a trio with Jack Bruce as featured vocalist.'

'There was no real notion about it at all,' recalls Hughie Flint, 'until we read about it in the *Melody Maker*. Actually what did happen was Ginger came down to a couple of gigs we played and sat in, which I was quite glad of – to sit out for a few numbers – and they were obviously incredible playing together, but unknown to us they were rehearsing at the same time. They'd been rehearsing for several weeks, if not a month or so, and it was all quiet because Ginger was working with Graham Bond, Jack was working with Manfred, and Eric was working with John. So they were trying to keep it hushed up, but it leaked out somewhere and it was reported in the paper. John and I were sat in his back garden, and John read this and was very displeased. I was very sad because it meant that Eric was going to leave, and I didn't know what was going to happen at all. Eric owned up and said, "I'd like to give a month's notice," and John said, "Fine." Then John met Peter Green two weeks later, and I don't remember much consultation, but he eventually turned round to Eric and said, "Well, you can leave tomorrow, because we've got another guitarist," so he actually fired Eric. There were several gigs towards the end of Eric's stay with the band where he just didn't turn up, so we played as a trio. It was pretty dire, but John insisted on carrying it off and getting paid and all the rest of it, but two solid hours of John Mayall, John McVie and myself must have been pretty heavy when most of the people wanted God.'

By the time the *Blues Breakers* album was released at the beginning of August, Cream were gigging. With an irony he could not have anticipated Neil Slaven wrote in his sleeve note, 'A lot of people wondered why Eric left the Yardbirds just as they were hitting big. But Eric had an inevitable course to follow, and at the time it led him to the Bluesbreakers, as no doubt it will lead him somewhere else in the future.' The reviews, as was perhaps to be expected of such an 'uncommercial' album, emphasized the *seriousness* of the project: 'John Mayall refuses to be sidetracked with minor issues like pop music or commercialization and is about the only group left in the country who ever claimed to play blues still actually playing that much-abused music. John's single-mindedness comes through in his approach to the organ, piano and harmonica, and to the material and its interpretation. It's all played relentlessly, bitingly and with feeling. There isn't a spark of humour in anybody's playing, be it John, Eric Clapton or any of the horn players added to a few tracks, John Almond (baritone), Alan Skidmore (tenor) and Dennis Healey (trumpet). It's joyless and savage and gives a grim satisfaction. No British musicians have ever sounded like this before on record. It is a giant step. It is a credit to John and his musicians.' There was no mention of the album's chart potential, though such prophecies were common in record reviews at the time; moreover, words like 'joyless' and 'grim satisfaction' did not make it sound much like a hit.

In fact, *Blues Breakers* was among the top ten albums within three weeks of its release and remained there throughout the autumn, which, Mike Vernon recalls, 'not only amazed Decca, it amazed me, to say the least it amazed John, who to this day I don't think believes that it was real, he still believes it was a dream. Looking at *Melody Maker* and seeing the album in the pop charts was all too much for him.'

Mayall hardly faltered as Peter Green replaced Clapton in the Bluesbreakers (nor did he when, later, Green was replaced by Mick Taylor), yet the period of his partnership with Clapton was unsurpassed by any of the constantly shifting, subsequent lineups. That year each won his reputation and laid the foundation for a renaissance of British blues. Alexis Korner, progenitor of the earlier R&B boom, acknowledged their contribution: 'During that time Mayall was building, and I thought Eric was playing incredibly at that time. I think that's the most incredible period of Clapton that I know. If you listen now to that album Eric made with John, there's some incredible guitar playing from Eric on that, quite, quite superb playing. That's where the blues renaissance built from – basically through John Mayall and Eric Clapton.'

Four

CREAM – THE GUITARIST AS SUPERHERO

Whenever it was that the term 'supergroup' was first used, it was surely in reference to Cream, without doubt the most influential band of the late sixties. Originally, however, they were described as a 'groups' group'.

Unconsciously anticipating the formation of such a group, *Melody Maker* had conducted a poll among current pop idols in March 1966 to elect an all-star line-up. Although it followed a conventional six-piece pattern of vocals, lead guitar, rhythm guitar, keyboards, bass and drums, Clapton was nominated as lead guitarist (by Mick Jagger, Eric Burdon, Steve Marriot and Paul Jones) and Ginger Baker as drummer (by Keith Moon, Paul Jones, the Merseys' Tony Crane and journalist Chris Welch). Jack Bruce was outvoted as bass guitarist by the Who's John Entwistle. Whether this dream team put the idea for Cream in Baker's head or not, it was shortly afterwards that he mentioned his project to Clapton. 'I was working in Graham Bond's band,' he told an interviewer, 'and Eric sat in a few times. He was working with John Mayall at Oxford – I drove to the gig and after sitting in, asked Eric if he would be prepared to join in a new band I was forming. He agreed and suggested we get Jack. I had every reason to say "No" as I had fired him from Bond's band six months before. But I agreed.' That he was prepared to play in the claustrophobic confines of a trio with someone he quite clearly couldn't get on with personally was a measure both of Baker's regard for Bruce's musicianship and of his desire to be in a band with Clapton.

Two weeks after the news of the group's formation in June 1966 it was announced that the trio had signed with Robert Stigwood. 'They will be called Cream,' Stigwood said, 'and will be represented by me for agency and management. They will record for my Reaction label and go into the studios next week to cut

tracks for their first single. Their debut will be at the National
Jazz and Blues Festival at Windsor in July, when their single will
be released.' Their chosen name was an arrogant and self-
conscious assessment of their own talents and of their status in
the British rock hierarchy, but no one argued with it.
The pedigree of both Bruce and Baker was lengthy and
impressive. Baker, a former trumpeter, had turned to drumming
in the fifties and risen through the growing ranks of the traditional jazz bands, among them Acker Bilk's and Terry Lightfoot's. A
residency at Ronnie Scott's jazz club followed, before he joined
Alexis Korner's newly formed Blues Incorporated in 1962 in
place of Charlie Watts. Jack Bruce had already joined the group
from Jim McHarg's Scotsville Jazzband, and the pair had in fact
met some months previously when Baker was with the Bert
Courtley Sextet. On that occasion they had immediately taken
to each other's playing. The Sextet's tenor player, Dick Heckstall-Smith, recalls, 'I was offered a jazz gig at the Cambridge
May Ball and, not having a group of my own, I asked Bert if I
could have his group for the night and use another trumpet
player. On this gig the band that was on in the same hall just
before us was Jim McHarg's Scotsville Jazzband. And the bass
player was short and very shy-looking and nervous and full of
movement. He asked me for a blow, and bass players from trad
bands often used to ask for blows and I used to discourage them,
so I said, "No, not now, but you can come back later to another
hall somewhere else." It was a basement at four o'clock in the
morning, and I thought that was the last I'd see of him, but he
turned up at four in the morning much to my surprise. I was very
pissed off, so I called a very, very fast blues, and Ginger and I
winked at each other and we made it very, very fast indeed – and
he played the arse off everyone. By the end of the number I was
knocked out, so I said, "Okay, next we'll do 'Lover Man' and you
play the tune," and he did. So me and Ginger latched on to him,
and when the time came in Alexis Korner's band when there was
some doubt about the rhythm section, I asked Jack to come
down for a blow at the Ealing Club, and he was in. Then Jack and
me asked Alexis if Ginger could come down for a blow, and he
played his arse off – and Charlie Watts offered to leave.' Bruce
and Baker remained with Blues Incorporated until February
1963 when they broke away with Graham Bond to form a quartet
with John McLaughlin, led by Bond. The band became the
Graham Bond Organization when McLaughlin was replaced by
Heckstall-Smith six months later, and the line-up remained the
same until Bruce quit towards the end of 1965. His short stint
with John Mayall's Bluesbreakers was followed by six months

with Manfred Mann, during which he played on the chart-topping single, 'Pretty Flamingo'.

The formation of Cream was an exceptional event in British rock history. As a rule groups were formed in all but local anonymity, and even when star members left well-known bands their replacements tended to be drawn from obscurity. Thus the advent of Cream created a great deal of excited anticipation for their debut at the Windsor Festival. Would the three be capable of subjugating their not inconsiderable egos to work in harness with their partners? Would their forceful and disparate styles synthesize successfully or blow themselves apart?

The intended musical direction of the group naturally aroused considerable interest. The jazz leanings of Bruce and Baker were, if not common knowledge, well known within musical circles, and looked likely to be at odds with, or perhaps even dominate, Clapton's single-minded pursuit of the blues. Interrupted at rehearsals in a village hall shortly before their first public appearance, they were asked about their intentions. Clapton said blues – 'ancient and modern' – and then, at Bruce's suggestion, 'sweet and sour rock and roll'. Asked if the music might not be a trifle jazzy, he was emphatic in his denial, insisting that jazz was 'definitely out' and adding, 'What we want to do is anything that people haven't done before. Pete Townshend is enthusiastic and he may write a number for us.... Most people have formed the impression of us as three solo musicians clashing with each other. We want to cancel that idea and be a group that plays together.'

At the Windsor Festival the crowd was predictably and uncritically ecstatic. As one observer put it, Clapton's playing 'induced the audience to shout and scream for more, even while he was playing more'. The mere presence of Clapton, Bruce and Baker on stage together would have been applauded, no matter what or how they played. As it was, their set included future Cream standards like the opener, 'Spoonful', Bruce's harmonica feature, 'Traintime', and Baker's drum solo, 'Toad'. However, a review of their next performance, at Cooks Ferry Inn in North London, failed to conceal disappointment, both on the part of the capacity crowd and the reporter: 'Enthusiastic shouting and cheering were reserved for the second half of their act when they dropped their nerves and reduced the gap between numbers. Solos from Eric, Ginger and Jack had the crowd in raptures, calling for more. Although Cream are still in the experimental stage, they are striving for a perfection which, when it does come, will be little short of sensational.'

Indeed, according to Ben Palmer, reunited with Clapton as

Cream's road manager, 'For a long time there was no suggestion
that we were ever going to be a very big band. We weren't going
out for very much money, the public interest was not great. It
was like every time Eric does anything new, there were more
people who were disappointed because they didn't hear what
they wanted him to do than there were who took immediately to
this new band, which was quite a shock to a lot of people. The
most striking thing in retrospect about Cream was that we
played to so many people without anybody getting especially
excited. It was ticking over: we got a single out, "Wrapping
Paper", which, I suppose, ticked over, and we got round to doing
some unlikely films for *Top Of The Pops*, dressed up as monks in
Richmond Park, and I remember getting a costume of Genghis
Khan for Ginger – which I thought was coals to Newcastle if ever
I'd heard of it – from Berman's. This sort of thing: the beginnings
of lavish presentation. It may be distorted by comparison with
what happened later, but I've always had the impression that we
worked very hard slogging round this country for a long time and
nothing much happened.'

'Wrapping Paper', released on 7 October, did nothing to re-
assure Clapton's fans. One reviewer wrote, 'Surprise surprise!
Their recording debut sees the Cream in a new light – and one
which will astound their fans – possibly even drive them to
suicide! ... Most disappointing is the musical content of the
number which is nil. It has obvious commerciality – might even
be a huge hit – but in the group's attempt at ultra-hipness and
shock treatment they may have outsmarted themselves.'

This opinion was borne out by poor sales. The record failed to
make the top twenty; ironically, at a time when the 'uncommercial' *Blues Breakers* album was enjoying its long and successful
run in the album charts. Clapton himself felt obliged to defend
the song: ' "Wrapping Paper" is an excuse, whatever people say,
for a twelve-bar blues. That's all it is. It's a good tune, and very
commercial, with the sort of feel that represents *us*! We do
exploit this kind of feeling – but retain the beaty feel as well.' But
the public remained unconvinced. It was the first product of the
songwriting partnership of Jack Bruce and poet/musician Pete
Brown and was essentially Bruce's record. It bore scant resemb-
lance to the rest of the group's repertoire and barely provided
Clapton with enough work to warm his fingers. Bruce and Brown
were, subsequently, to more than make amends. The most
encouraging sign was the record's B-side, which featured a
powerful reworking of Doctor Ross' 'Cat's Squirrel'. This was
certainly more familiar ground for both Clapton and his followers.

Fears that Clapton might be setting out in a new direction were not alleviated by his own statements. In October, shortly after the release of 'Wrapping Paper', he announced: 'My whole musical attitude has changed. I listen to the same sounds and records but with a different ear. I'm no longer trying to play anything but like a white man. The time is overdue when people should play like they are and what colour they are. I don't believe I've ever played so well in my life. More is expected of me in the Cream – I have to play rhythm guitar as well as lead.... Sure I've changed. Jack Bruce has had a tremendous influence on my playing – and my personality. It's a lot easier to play in a blues band than in a group where you've got to play purely your own, individual ideas. You have got to put over a completely new kind of music – this needs a different image. Jack, Ginger and I have absorbed a lot of music, and now we're trying to produce our own music – which naturally incorporates many things you've heard, and many ideas you've had. It's hard. It's also original. It's also more satisfying, and a lot more worthwhile.'

For Clapton's fans, especially those who did not have an opportunity to see the group perform, these first months of Cream were confusing. An album, scheduled for release in late October (supposedly to be followed by an EP of Christmas carols in December!), was postponed, and, as if offering a more physical threat to the group's future, Ginger Baker collapsed several times on stage during performances.

However, by November the group, who had undoubtedly been under-rehearsed when they first appeared in public, were playing with greater fluency and rapport, as a report of a performance at Klooks Kleek confirmed: 'Any doubts about the Cream's ability to perform as a group and not just three star soloists were dispelled by their sensational set. In fact one of their main strengths proved to be the fantastic empathy that exists between them. Reports have been filtering in of bad performances by the Cream, but there they were seen to be obviously enjoying each other's playing tremendously, and working together like a team of bomb disposal experts. Eric Clapton played one of the most outstanding solos of his career on "Steppin' Out", which he sustained for minutes on end. Ginger Baker battered fill-ins and off-beats with frightening ferocity, and Jack Bruce rivalled Eric's virtuosity with an incredible harmonica solo on "Traintime" and "Rolling And Tumbling". Eric sang with feeling and Jack's bass playing was as fast and powerful as the Flying Scotsman. Here is one of the most musically rewarding and fascinating groups making it today, and if anybody should record a "live" LP it's the Cream.'

In fact, Cream's first album, when it eventually appeared in December, was very much a studio recording and as such the first clear indication of the disparity that constantly existed between the group's work on stage and in the studio. Taken away from the high energy atmosphere of their live performances into the controlled environment of the recording studio, few of the numbers that had already become favourites with their audiences retained their power. Ginger Baker's drum feature, 'Toad', especially, was quite pointless in a situation where he was his sole stimulus, apart from the silent faces behind the glass panel of the control box. Half the album's material was made up of the expected blues standards, two of which – Willie Dixon's 'Spoonful' and Skip James' 'I'm So Glad' – reappeared on later albums as memorable (and much extended) live recordings. The original material that filled the remaining tracks was fundamentally weak, owing largely to the indisposition of Jack Bruce's songwriting partner, Pete Brown, who, as he later admitted, had 'got into such a bad state, I had to stop everything'.

By the time *Fresh Cream* was released the group had themselves grown dissatisfied with it. Shortly afterwards Clapton said, 'I am not happy about it as it could have been better. We were working on it so long ago and we have greatly improved since then. I'm not completely happy with the production.' At least one reviewer agreed with Clapton that the record had not been helped by its delay, when he wrote, 'At last off the presses, but not quite as fresh as it could have been. The Cream are the kind of group who are progressing all the time and though this album was recorded recently it's already almost early material.' The public, however, having waited six months since the formation of the group, were undeterred. By the end of January the album was in the top five, where it remained for some weeks.

A single, 'I Feel Free' (backed by 'NSU'), was issued to coincide with *Fresh Cream* and gave the group a top twenty hit. In spite of an unexpected section of acapella vocals, the record was altogether less quirky than 'Wrapping Paper' and featured prominently the distinctive sustain technique which Clapton referred to as 'woman tone' and which confused one reviewer of 'I Feel Free' enough to suggest it 'could either be feedback, organ or a theremin'.

It might seem hard to believe, given the effects available to guitarists in the eighties, but back in 1966 a lot of people didn't know how the hell Clapton created some of the sounds that came out of his Gibson Les Paul by way of a Marshall amp. Fans would pester the music press for information, journalists would theorize, Clapton himself attempted explanations, but hearing how wasn't the half of it.

What came across in a classic Clapton solo was much more than technique. There had been fast fingered guitarists before him in rock, players with impressive dexterity, but Clapton could hold one note, bend it, stretch it to a scream, and make an audience's eyes moist with emotion, such was the intensity of the feeling he put into it. Previously only certain singers had held that power, but in Clapton's hands a guitar spoke soul to soul.

The schizophrenic nature of Cream's first recordings is directly related to the fact that they were made so soon after the group's inception, before the trio's intentions were firmly defined. Clapton's original concept had been a three-piece 'like Buddy Guy with a rhythm section', but lack of rehearsals before their first gigs left them short of material and thus obliged to fill out their set by improvising, though not to the extent they did later. Their affection for a muted form of dadaism, as manifested in 'Wrapping Paper' and bizarre stage costumes, soon sank from sight and only resurfaced in aberrant isolation on later albums. There had, quite simply, been no specific group strategy before Cream first went on stage. 'We had decided we wanted to play with each other more than anyone else in the country,' Clapton said a year later, 'and formed a band. Completely co-operative. We just did it. It wasn't very hard, it was easy. Putting it together was hard because we had no idea what we really wanted to play, we just knew we wanted to play together. We had no idea of what material we wanted to do and for a long time it was hard to find a real direction.'

By the start of 1967, however, a certain stability had been established and, in the minds of Clapton, Bruce and Baker, at least, a clear, if barely articulated aim. As Clapton put it at the time, 'We are still knocking each other out and that's enough. After the early criticisms we have got through to audiences, and what really surprises us is that not only do fans welcome the blues things, they like the things Jack has written as well. They like our whole programme.... We just haven't torn each other to pieces and things are swinging along beautifully. It's the only group where we all work to knock each other out as well as the audience ... I think the reason we have been accepted is because everything else has been done now. People have seen everybody and now their minds are wide open. It's a completely open market.' Ginger Baker was equally optimistic: 'It's a progression and it will go on, as we are doing something different all the time. I think it's a load of crap when people say we aren't working out as a group. We have had some plays that have been absolutely tremendous. We draw big crowds and they thoroughly enjoy themselves. We are three totally different personalities and none of us think alike, but we get more and more together musically. It's world class in my opinion, and I don't think there are three other musicians about to touch it.'

The notion of playing for *themselves* as much as for their audience was unfamiliar within the field of rock music, especially in public performance where a stage act was still expected of a successful group. Arguably, few groups possessed the necessary skills or inventiveness in improvisation to allow such self-indulgence. In Cream both existed in abundance.

The key word in their credo was Baker's: progression. Progression beyond what groups had done before; progression beyond the blues. And as long as the urge to create was present, Cream were genuinely progressive. By the seventies, as imitators sweated in the space created by their break-up, like so many punch-drunk prize fighters, 'progressive' had become an absurd and inaccurate epithet, for in those second- and third-generation progressive groups there was unquestionably no progression.

But Cream, having mastered the blues, moved on. In mid-1967 Clapton told a reporter, 'I don't think I really represent the blues any more. Not truly. I have more of that in me and my music than anything else, but I don't really play blues any more.' His plans for Cream, he said, were 'nothing more ambitious than being as musically free as we can. You can't even guess where that will take you musically. I don't know where I'll be in the next year.'

One area in which Clapton himself was anxious to progress was the extension of the technical possibilities of the guitar. Having, as he put it, 'got to the point now where my playing satisfies me technically,' he was ready to experiment with 'a few new recording effects and … a few ideas for the guitar'.

The opportunity to experiment in the recording studio arose at the end of the group's first trip to America in April, where they played the teen-oriented Murray The K Show at the RKO theatre in New York for ten days. Ben Palmer recalls, 'It was a big bill, a lot of acts, and it was supposed to be five shows a day. I think the first curtain was at ten o'clock in the morning – the kids were on holiday – and the last show would go on not far short of midnight, and that was for the supper crowd coming out of the theatres. There was Wilson Pickett, Simon and Garfunkel, the Blues Project, the Cream, the Who and umpteen other people. It was utter chaos from beginning to end and not a striking success of any kind. One number, "I'm So Glad", five times a day, it had to be the same, had to have the quote from the "Marseillaise", shouldn't necessarily go much over three minutes, put on all kinds of psychedelic costumes at enormous cost, instruments still tacky with paint at the first show, and nothing approaching anything that you could call success – just another job finished and time to go home. In fact, the band was so low at the end of it, that I seem to remember that special arrangements were made for them to go into Atlantic and do an LP just to let them get down to something that wasn't so clearly a travesty of their intentions and their interests. That was what this show was, an utterly unsuitable thing for them ever to have done, and I'm pretty sure that they very much rushed through the plans for making an LP at Atlantic to restore the band's confidence, it was so low at the time. They came home feeling very much better for it, I think.'

The sessions at Atlantic's New York studios produced Cream's second album, *Disraeli Gears*. Although it was not released until November, two tracks, 'Strange Brew' and 'Tales Of Brave Ulysses', were lifted as a single at the end of May. 'Strange Brew' was as much Clapton's record as 'Wrapping Paper' had been Jack Bruce's, since he wrote it (with Felix Pappalardi) and sang it as well as playing guitar. It was basically a blues number, adapted through its psychedelic lyrics, frail, dreamy vocals, and a hovering, stinging guitar line over crashing chord punctuation, to a precisely contemporary context. And it went perfectly with his new hairstyle, an extravagant afro of a perm worn in imitation of Bob Dylan. A lot of kids soon shaved off their sideboards and moustaches, and turned curly instead, and they discarded their military jackets in favour of kaftans and beads. Clapton could never understand why people who liked the sound of his guitar needed to look like him.

Commercially, 'Strange Brew' was less successful than 'I Feel Free' had been. It entered the top twenty in the second week of July, but climbed no higher than fourteenth place. Later in the year, Clapton announced the group's intention to ignore singles: 'What we're doing now is simply concentrating on LPs. And if by accident a single should come out of an LP session, then we'll put it on the market. Whereas before you'd have two sessions; you'd consciously go to an LP session or you'd consciously go to a single session. And single sessions are terrible. I can't make them at all. They're just like – you go in there and the whole big problem is whether it's commercial. That is the problem. No matter what the music is like, it's got to be commercial, it's got to have a hook line, you've got to have this and that and you just fall into a very dark hole. I can't take it at all.'

Though unappreciated by singles buyers, Cream were treated more kindly by the readers of *Melody Maker*, who voted the trio fourth best British group (after the Beatles, the Rolling Stones and the Jimi Hendrix Experience, all of whom had enjoyed considerably greater chart success than Cream that year) in the annual pop poll. Clapton himself did even better, winning the British musician section – a pat on the back, but not enough to convince Clapton or Cream that their future lay in the UK. According to Jack Bruce, 'The thing was that it just wasn't really happening in England, we were stagnating in a way because we hadn't got over certain gaps. And there was a limit in what you could do if you didn't get beyond a certain point, so we were going to split the group up.'

In September 1967 they set out on their first full-scale American tour, with the memory of those disastrous New York dates still vivid enough to cause concern. 'We expected that it would be the same kind of thing,' Bruce recalled, 'nobody knowing us and wanting to know us. The first place we played was the Fillmore – the old Fillmore in San Francisco – and we got there and we played and it was amazing, because the whole place had come to see us. It was a good bill. The Electric Flag had just formed, and it was embarrassing because we went down so well that the whole audience left and didn't bother to wait for the Electric Flag, and so they split up. We'd just been doing three, four, five-minute versions of our songs before we went out to San Francisco, and we were very, very nervous because this was something really big for us and also it was almost the first time we had played to a full house. But all these kids had actually come to see us and it was the first time we'd had our own audience on that scale, and they were just shouting out things like, "Just play anything, just play, we love you" and stuff, and the whole thing ended up with us just playing these incredibly long improvised things. We became known for that, I suppose, and that was how it started, and it was also the best time for the group.'

As Clapton put it at the time, 'We seem to be a lot more popular here than I imagined. I knew that we had been heard of through the underground thing, yet I didn't imagine we'd be this popular.' San Francisco was certainly the right place to make it in 1967; the city's aura that summer was like Liverpool's four years before, and the ovation of the Fillmore crowd was effectively a universally recognized seal of approval. This was what the group had been working for, hoping for. Back in New York they put in more time at Atlantic's studios. Then, in October, Cream returned to Britain, their reputation fortified by American success.

Disraeli Gears was released and became an instant hit,

although it failed to climb higher than fifth place in a chart that had been dominated for six months by the Beatles' *Sergeant Pepper's Lonely Hearts Club Band*. The result of the sessions which had taken place in New York six months earlier, its foundations had less to do with the blues than with the spirit of 1967. Apart from 'Strange Brew', the blues influence was only apparent in 'Outside Woman Blues', which was also sung by Clapton, and the lighthearted 'Take It Back'. If his playing on these tracks was familiar, elsewhere Clapton employed a formidable array of styles and technical effects. The inspiration behind this break away from a blues-based approach was undoubtedly Jimi Hendrix, who had virtually rewritten the rulebook since his arrival in London the previous year, and Clapton's enterprise was merited by a strong collection of songs (ignoring the throwaway 'Mother's Lament', performed like a barroom singsong, and 'Blue Condition', a Ginger Baker dirge so leaden it undermined his later complaint that Bruce and Clapton unfairly overlooked his compositions).

'Sunshine Of Your Love' was classic Cream. Even without Pete Brown's elegant lyrics or the poignant vocal duet between Bruce and Clapton or the guitarists' wistful solo, it would have remained an indelible piece of rock graffiti, splashed on a million memories, because its basis was the definitive heavy metal riff. In inventing it, Cream ultimately had a lot to answer for, since it begat a thousand bastards – mostly an obnoxious lot. Not that Eric, Jack or Ginger were to know that.

In contrast, 'Dance The Night Away' (Bruce/Brown), with its West Coast origins and distorted mandolinesque guitar, and 'Tales Of Brave Ulysses' (Clapton/Sharp), where Hendrix's fingerprints showed up all over the frets, were as psychedelic as Martin Sharp's bewildering sleeve collage. On Bruce's atmospheric 'We're Going Wrong', Clapton held back for more than half the number then drifted in like scented smoke and hung there, haunting, till the end.

Bruce, throughout, sang with control, exalted the role of bass guitarist. Baker stayed under the spell and not once turned into the Toad.

Inevitably, the success in America which put Cream at their peak created a situation which first exhausted and then finally suffocated the group. During the period which immediately preceded the British release of *Disraeli Gears* and the weeks that followed, they played a string of successful dates in England, including a notable performance at London's Saville Theatre.

But however strong the group's desire to play to the British public or retain contact with their audiences in small venues, there was no doubting where the dollars were. It was clear that if they undertook long tours of America, Cream could clean up.

Although the Beatles had opened America for British groups in 1964, that first wave of the British Invasion had been an assault on the pop charts and adolescent hearts. On stage in the States the groups were only going through the motions, allowing America's teens the opportunity to scream and toss jelly beans at their idols from England whose hits they already had at home, and the main reward was money – like the 180,000 dollars the Beatles earned at New York's Shea Stadium on an August evening in 1965 – because there was no creative satisfaction to be had from doing half an hour of hits that couldn't be heard above the hysteria. And the hits always came first; without one there was no reason to book a transatlantic ticket.

The Beatles' last concert in San Francisco's Candlestick Park in August 1966, more than a year before Cream's first date in the same city, signalled the end of the first phase of the British Invasion. They returned to the UK, withdrew into the special sanctum of EMI's Abbey Road studio, and made their most imaginative music. Cream did it differently. There had been no hits. They earned their reputation on the road, bettering their studio performances on stage.

In February 1968 they began an American tour that was due to last several months. Early in April it was announced that the tour had been extended until July: the longest tour ever by a British group. Within a fortnight they were back in England for an unexpected ten-day break, while Robert Stigwood emphatically dismissed rumours that the group was breaking up. 'Nothing,' he said, with more faith than foresight, 'could be further from the truth.' And, after admitting that the schedule he had arranged was too intensive, explained that the cancelled dates would be tacked onto the tour's end.

Interviewed during his stay, Clapton backed up his manager's statement: 'All the rumours are denied. I'm happy with the group, although needless to say there has been strain. We've been doing two and a half months of one-nighters and that is the hardest I have ever worked in my life. Financially and popularity-wise we're doing unbelievably well in America.... All rumours denied! I mean – the group isn't going to last for ever, but it's not going to break up in the foreseeable future. If we hadn't had this holiday we might have broken up anyway. We all know where it's at in the group. Each one of us has got to be free to move. We've just got over a period of recording inactivity and we have two

LPs out soon, one recorded "live" at the Fillmore and one in the studio, which will boost our ego and give us more confidence. I've been feeling tired and frustrated.'

In spite of Stigwood's confidence and Clapton's own PR job for Cream, the rumours persisted. The strain of such protracted touring would surely take its toll; and strain there was by the bellyful. Tour manager Ben Palmer recalls, 'The reason there were pressures then is because no one had ever done it before. Nobody had tried to keep this sort of schedule and lead this kind of life, that anybody knew – though I suppose bands like Count Basie and Ellington and that had been doing it for half a century. Of course, it'd been done, but not by people like us. And we had no idea what facilities there were, how to use them, we had no idea what was going to happen. You could look at a pile of contracts and guess what some of the problems might be, but you couldn't possibly have guessed what the atmosphere was like and what the involvement really meant to you personally after a few weeks. Whatever pressures arose came because we were totally unprepared for any of it, and that's nobody's fault, nobody could have been prepared. They didn't result in internal pressures in the band to start off with, and it's very hard to say when you're not one of the band why the difficulties arise that do arise, but I think it would be fairest to everybody who was in the band to say that the pressures of touring were only a catalyst. It was only a background to the conflicts that did inevitably arise and which were dealt with, modified, developed. It wasn't just always: Oh, Ginger and Eric don't get on, or Jack and Ginger are always fighting and so on. There were all sorts of arguments throughout that very intense period of working and living together just as you would expect any group of people to encounter, and certainly the pressures of touring provided a very fertile background for that sort of thing to breed in, but I don't think that caused it.'

Strangely perhaps, the pressures throughout that marathon of one-nighters did not, according to Palmer, directly affect the group's performances. 'They remained,' he says, 'quite unpredictable and were sometimes as fresh as for the first time, and I could never detect what brought that about. Circumstances could be very adverse to a good performance and yet a good performance would happen. I came to decide that it was something within the band, it was something between the three people within the band – and that and only that. It didn't ever seem to bear any relationship to outside pressures or favourable circumstances. You could take your time, have three or four days off and really get a long way away from music, please yourself, a good venue, a pleasant promoter, a nice hotel, everything going smoothly, and a really rotten performance – not really rotten, because they never did get bad, but a very ordinary performance. It didn't seem to affect the band, it was a purely internal matter, purely internal chemistry that would ever account for the way they played. I came to decide that; I had to really, because it would otherwise have confused me too utterly. I naturally tried to make every job as easy to play as possible – whatever it required to have the band go on stage feeling good, but it was frequently so insufficient that you could only conclude that the band existed very much with a privacy of its own. With a band like Cream there is a privacy about it which nobody penetrates. And it's within that that you would find the reason for any variance in the performances, rather than the touring pressures.'

Commenting on the impenetrability of bands, Clapton confirms, 'It's like a secret society. Doing an interview there's certain things I'm not prepared to divulge. There's a certain part of me which is an allegiance to those fellers which I can't tell even the missus about, because either it wouldn't interest her or it's none of her business – it covers every aspect: humour, tragedy, whatever you like. And you can't crack that. Even another musician can't crack it. You can go and jam with a group like that and 'you're still standing on the outside even though you're right there on stage with them making the same amount of noise – you're not anything to do with them at all. Once it's been there, it never dies.'

In May it was announced that Cream would tour Britain on their return from America in July. 'The tour,' a spokesman said, 'dispels all rumours of the group splitting up.' But it didn't, and by the time Cream arrived back in England, the rumours had been confirmed. The group was to break up at the end of the year after a farewell tour of America, due to start in October, and a solitary performance at the Albert Hall. Not unnaturally, Robert Stigwood stressed that the break was amicable and that the three were splitting up purely in order to 'follow their individual musical policies'. Such bland assertions offered scant comfort to the group's British fans, one of whom wrote to *Melody Maker*: 'So the Cream are breaking up. We were wondering if they still existed. What are we getting as a last farewell? One lousy concert.

'Goodbye Eric, Jack and Ginger. We dug your sound, but you kicked us in the teeth.'

A few weeks later, after the release of Cream's double album, Ginger Baker said, 'If you listen to *Wheels Of Fire* there are none of Eric's things on it, which is wrong. What it boils down to is we

Above: The Roosters, 1963: (l. to r.) Eric Clapton, Robin Mason, Terry Brennan, Tom McGuinness, Ben Palmer

Left: The Yardbirds, 1964

Below: The Yardbirds, 1964: (l. to r.) Jim McCarty, Chris Dreja, Keith Relf, Paul Samwell-Smith, Eric Clapton

Left: Giorgio
Gomelsky

Right: Robert
Stigwood

Far right: John
Mayall

Below: Cream
rehearsing for 'Ready
Steady Go', 1966

Above and bottom right: Clapton in Cream

Left: Blind Faith rehearsing at Eric's, 1969: (l. to r.) Steve Winwood, Rick Grech, Ginger Baker, Eric Clapton

Right: Derek and the Dominos, 1970: (l. to r.) Jim Gordon, Carl Radle, Bobby Whitlock, Eric Clapton and Jeep

Above: Rainbow concert, 1973:
(l. to r.) Rick Grech, Eric Clapton,
Pete Townshend

Left: April 1974

Philadelphia sound check, 1974

Left: 1983
Below: Patti and Eric, 1983

all like to write and get our musical ideas across, and it seems the only way we can do this is separately. I've talked to a few people about this. There is a rift. In America, me and Eric had the idea of knocking it on the head, but I was still a bit surprised it came out so soon, because we are still working to the end of the year. I think he's been feeling frustrated. All our records have been good, but material has been a problem. The best number we did was "Tales Of Brave Ulysses". The potential, especially Eric's, is ridiculous. There are more things that should be played and written.'

Jack Bruce went further: 'I think it was the usual reason. Everybody wants to exploit themselves individually. I think if we did go on the same way, there wasn't anywhere else we could progress as a group. The only thing we could have done was play to more and more people in more places ... I think we made some sort of progress, but the first time we went to the States we reached a peak. The first time at the Fillmore we seemed to get it all together and stayed like that until the last concert we did. The [last] tour had a double-edged effect. One was to make us very popular, the other was to make us uptight about the group. I had a lot in me that wouldn't have come out [without Cream]. The singing and the songwriting. Suddenly I was the lead singer of a group that was very successful. It was a shock.... We got certain things from it apart from financial gain. Eric's guitar playing has improved tremendously, especially his time. He used to play everything in neat four-time phrases but he's really improved. His time has got incredible now, and, as I say, it brought out my singing and songwriting, I suppose.... If we'd stayed in England, we possibly wouldn't have stayed together as long as we did. When we went to the States we found we could just wail and the audiences would dig it. It was a nice feeling.'

And John Mayall added another opinion. 'I know Eric pretty well,' he said. 'From the beginning I could see it would be good for him for a short while, but it became a money-making combine and that's not Eric's scene at all. I don't know if Eric will ever play again. He basically doesn't like playing for people. I think he will go into recording and make fewer appearances.'

'The Cream,' said Clapton himself succinctly, 'has lost direction.' But elsewhere and at other times he expressed different views. Certainly he resented the strain and constrictions of incessant tours, which turned the trio in on themselves and directed all their energies towards only one goal – the next performance – away from experimentation, from new material, away even from rehearsal. Also he had grown weary of keeping the peace between Bruce and Baker, who, in spite of their

musical harmony, had soon renewed the personal enmity that
had earlier forced Bruce out of the Graham Bond Organization.
Like Bruce he felt the group had reached a peak the previous
year in San Francisco, but he was more ready than Bruce to
point out the subsequent decline into mere virtuosity. 'From
that [the Fillmore concerts] we all went on such a huge ego trip.
Making it in the States was a bang on the head.... With the
Cream solos were the thing, but I'm really off that virtuoso kick.
It was all over exposed.' Years later he recounted an apocryphal
story about a gig where he had stopped playing halfway through
a number and Bruce and Baker had carried on unnoticing to the
end. Even allowing for the exaggeration of memory and ill-
feeling (if any still lingered) the anecdote underlines the self-
indulgence that marked the group's excesses of bravura.

There were, too, outside influences that prompted Clapton's
decision to announce the end of Cream. He had begun to hanker
after a more flexible line-up than bare guitar/bass/drums. He
wanted keyboards and he wanted a new approach. And he
wanted a new role for himself. 'I want to be in a group where I can
control the music,' he said, 'but I want to be at the back.' The
decisive factor had been hearing a tape of the Band's first album,
Music From Big Pink. The egoless unity of their playing and the
strength of the album's songs without a heroic solo in earshot
tipped the scales. He realized what he wanted, and he wanted it
now.

That tape marked a turning point he remembered vividly a
decade later. 'I got hold of a bootleg tape of *Big Pink* from
somewhere at the end of the last Cream tour – or the one before
the farewell tour – and I used to take it and put it on as soon as I
checked in to my hotel room and listen to it and *then go and do
the gig* and be utterly miserable, and then rush back and put the
tape on and go to sleep fairly contented until I woke up the next
morning and remembered who I was and what I was doing. It
was *that* potent! I don't think the *Big Pink* album sold particularly well or anything – it was very much a closed shop. It wasn't
publicly exposed the same way it was to musicians, and it had a
shocking effect on more people than you can actually ever
realize. The sound of music changed drastically after that first
album – everywhere.

'I had to go and *see* what they looked like right after I got *Big
Pink*, so I went up to Woodstock and visited, and they just
turned out to be great people – very intelligent, very tight. And I
was in awe of them ever since.'

The fickle power of the rock press affected him as well;
crucially, the juxtaposition in *Rolling Stone* of Jann Wenner's

lengthy and deferential interview and a concert review which dismissed him as 'the master of the cliche'. He has remained distrustful of the press ever since.

Having made up his mind and made it public, having been advised and abused, and having hinted at his intentions to form a new group – 'I've already had plays with a few people,' he revealed in July, 'and I know the musicians I want ... I'll start work on the new group in November' – he was stuck for a while at least with his obligations to Cream. A single, 'Anyone For Tennis', had been released in May and died an entirely appropriate death. Written and sung by Clapton, it was pop at its most lightweight and forgettable, and made nonsense of his declaration of a few weeks before: 'You get really hung up and try to write pop songs and create a pop image. I went through that stage and it was a shame because I was not being true to myself. I am and always will be a blues guitarist.' Apparently intended originally for inclusion on the group's next album, it did not reappear.

In August the double album *Wheels Of Fire* was released. It was ironic that Cream's most definitive statement on record should only be heard at a time when they were on the point of breaking up and for many British fans the live set on sides three and four would be their only opportunity to hear the group performing in their most characteristic style. Curiously, the studio set that comprised the first two sides was released separately in the same month (as was the live set in December); both the double and single albums were hits.

What was immediately striking about *Wheels Of Fire* was the absence of any songs by Eric Clapton. Of the nine studio tracks, four were written by Jack Bruce and Pete Brown and three by Ginger Baker and Mike Taylor; the other two were blues, Howlin' Wolf's 'Sitting On Top Of The World' and Booker T. Jones and William Bell's 'Born Under A Bad Sign'. Furthermore Clapton hardly sang at all – nothing more than a couple of vocal harmonies. The dominant figure throughout was Bruce. Besides singing and playing bass, he added cello to several numbers, including 'As You Said', which was virtually a solo performance augmented only by Baker's high hat, acoustic guitars, recorder and calliope. Often Clapton's playing was indistinct except when he unleashed solos of furious power.

Nevertheless, the studio album contained some of Cream's finest work. Apart from the drummer's dire monologue, 'Pressed Rat And Warthog', the material was well up to scratch, which was to be expected of the Bruce/Brown compositions, but not Baker's. His past songwriting form could only have encouraged unreasonable optimists to anticipate such well-constructed numbers as 'Passing The Time' and 'Those Were The Days', the second of which featured a quite unexpectedly manic guitar solo from Clapton. The two blues tracks, presumably, were Clapton's contributions, even though they were sung by Bruce, but his playing on both was most notable for its lack of urgency. His most dynamic work he reserved for the three Bruce/Brown songs: 'White Room', where his incisive use of wahwah antici-pated the searing passage on Blind Faith's 'Presence Of The Lord'; 'Politician', with its ponderous, menacing bass riff and deliberately confused multi-tracked solo; and 'Deserted Cities Of The Heart', which he pushed to the very edge with a vibrant solo of harsh, trembling power. It is a measure of the strength of the live set, rather than any flaws in the studio sides, that these tracks were eclipsed by the Fillmore recordings.

It was never more evident than on *Wheels Of Fire* that Cream were two entirely different bands. Their aims in the arenas of recording studio and stage were quite separate. According to Ben Palmer, 'It was pretty clear in the studio that what the band did on stage was something which was left outside. This was a different kind of work and it was treated very differently and thought about quite differently. Jack, especially, he belonged to two bands really: one on stage and one for recording. And the others were quite happy with that. They were a band that worked so much with and for the audience that it would have been crazy to have done that sort of thing in the studio without an audience, not to talk about impossible. It would actually have been sort of mad, really. Pointless.'

The 'Live At The Fillmore' set was, quite simply, a record of Cream working with and for an audience: a consolation prize for everyone who had never seen and never would see the group on stage, and a memento for all those who had. The next-best-thing to being there.

In 'Crossroads' it froze four of the most exhilarating minutes of the band's career. That version of Robert Johnson's blues was a startling consummation of their talents, and within the genre that they themselves created it has overshadowed all else. Based on a solid twelve-bar foundation, it builds from a series of verses, each split by a riff like a buzz saw, into two solos of towering construction, the second a pinnacle of rock guitar. Throughout, Clapton was constantly prodded and harassed by Bruce, borne along by Baker's relentless rhythm. Even if he'd never played another note, there would have been nothing left to prove.

If 'Crossroads' was Clapton's masterpiece, Bruce and Baker made sure they had their share of the spotlight. Bruce's showpiece was a harmonica feature – just as his harp battle with Paul Jones had been during his stint with Manfred Mann. 'Traintime' was undeniably clever and whatever limitations it did have were those of the harmonica itself as a solo instrument. It was followed by Baker's mammoth 'Toad', a drum solo approached with such vigour that Baker would occasionally pass out at its conclusion. He once described his approach to it. 'I think the way I play,' he said, 'as well as being musical, is very athletic. I use all my limbs. I get near to a blackout every night after the solo and sometimes I can't stand up. I play the solo to a pattern so that the others know when to come in, but I try to do something new every time. I never play the same solo twice, but if you're playing with a band, you've got to play to a pattern ... I like to get excited by the drums before I play the climax.' Naturally affected by the vagaries of mood and situation, his lengthy solos were inconsistent, but on a good night he could sustain the audience's interest for fifteen minutes in a way few rock drummers have been able to. On record, and on this occasion, it flagged.

However, the key to the live album, and to Cream's performances on stage generally, was 'Spoonful'. Like 'Traintime' and 'Toad', Willie Dixon's blues standard had been included in their first public appearance at the Windsor Festival two years before and had remained a cornerstone of the group's repertoire ever since.

Starting out from its devastatingly simple pivotal riff and a perfunctory sequence of verse/chorus/verse/chorus, they progressed rapidly into extended improvisation, tied to the central theme by a thread so thin it soon became invisible. All that counted from that point on was whatever flowed between Clapton, Bruce and Baker, and between them and their audience. Heard first time on record it was mightily impressive, but inevitably it eventually lost its spontaneity. The cracks began to show through; those moments of uncertainty, of briefly lost direction, which in live performance were concealed by the overwhelming rush of energy from the stage, jabbed the ears on record. It remained, none the less, a giant testimony to a unique group.

In September Cream and Clapton consolidated their positions in *Melody Maker*'s pop poll. The group was voted third in British and international sections behind the Beatles and the Stones, and Clapton top musician in both categories. But around the same time disc jockey John Peel recounted an incident which underlined the ambiguity of Clapton's adulation. 'I can't say that I know Eric very well,' he admitted with characteristic modesty, 'but he does seem to find blind acceptance unattractive. I thought the reaction to him at Sunbury Festival was very interesting. When he walked out to play with Ginger Baker, unannounced, they clapped politely and thought: "Nice guitarist." When he was announced – yells and thunderous applause.' The public was listening to *him* rather than his guitar. As early as October 1966, he had remarked of Cream's British audiences, 'I don't believe we'll ever get over to them. People will always listen with biased ears, look through unbelieving eyes, and with preconceived ideas, remembering what we used to be, and so on.' Being a guitar hero could be a bringdown.

Another small but significant event which occurred in September was the release of 'Sunshine Of Your Love' and 'Swlabr' from *Disraeli Gears* as a single. ('White Room'/'Those Were The Days', the only *Wheels Of Fire* single, was not released until January 1969.) A minor hit – it barely scraped into the UK top thirty, although it had sold a million in America – it was the first sign of the relentless reshuffling and repackaging of Cream records that went on after their demise.

By this time Clapton had begun an association with the Beatles' George Harrison that led immediately to sessions for Jackie Lomax's 'Sour Milk Sea' (as Eddie Clayton, with Harrison on acoustic guitar, Nicky Hopkins on piano, and Ringo Starr), Harrison's *Wonderwall* film score, the shimmeringly beautiful 'While My Guitar Gently Weeps' on the Beatles' 'white' album, and subsequently to other collaborations. It also threw him together with Harrison's wife Patti with whom he would fall in love.

In October, less than a week after the start of Cream's farewell American tour, the British music press carried a story that briefly rekindled the hopes of the group's disappointed fans. Their manager, Robert Stigwood, was flying to the States at once in order to 'talk over again their plan to disband at the end of the year'. He explained, 'I have given a great deal of thought to the possibility of Eric Clapton, Jack Bruce and Ginger Baker staying together and I shall try and persuade them to do so.' In any case, whatever the outcome of his visit, there would be more records. At least six American concerts had been recorded for possible release, and studio time had been booked in New York at the end of the tour and in London on their return to lay down tracks for a final album.

On 26 October at the Albert Hall Cream played their last date, although Clapton was moved to admit afterwards that their reception by both houses – a second show had been added when the first sold out in two hours – had given them 'second thoughts about breaking up, but it would be unfair to change everybody's plans now'. Their set contained no surprises, but a selection of favourites that included 'White Room', 'I'm So Glad', 'Sitting On Top Of The World', 'Crossroads', 'Toad', 'Sunshine Of Your Love' and 'Steppin' Out'. Film cameras were there to record the event for posterity and a screening on BBC 2's *Omnibus* on 5 January. Clapton seemed genuinely surprised at their popularity. 'We haven't played here for – well I don't know how long – over a year, and I had no idea we were so popular. I was amazed we played to such full houses. I didn't think anybody would remember us.... It was really a fine evening for me, and I felt very excited. Before I went on I was as nervous as I've ever been. I always remember English audiences as being rather cold, yet they were so great.'

If the concert marked the close of the group's performing career, it did not mean an end to their records. They completed their *Goodbye* album in December and it was released at the beginning of March 1969 in a week when their first album had returned to the charts. In belated appreciation their fans made it their biggest hit. It entered the charts in second place in mid-March and a fortnight later was at No. 1, where it remained for a total of five weeks.

Like *Wheels Of Fire* it was an amalgam of live and studio tracks, though, because the live material spilled over onto the second side, there was only room for three studio tracks. Each of the three live numbers had appeared on previous Cream albums as studio cuts: 'I'm So Glad' on *Fresh Cream*, 'Politician' and 'Sitting On Top Of The World' on *Wheels Of Fire*. The quality and energy of the playing effectively dispelled any notion that Cream's chemistry had turned sterile during their last days together. The formula remained as secretly magical as alchemy to the end. Although 'Politician' sounded unnervingly stark without the multiple tracks of the recording studio that had provided much of its force, both 'I'm So Glad' and 'Sitting On Top Of The World' had grown in strength. On the first Clapton played like a river in flood, an unstoppable torrent of notes which swept the listener along on its hurtling current to the eventual calm of his and Bruce's repetition of the title refrain in vocal harmony; and in place of the relaxed, almost weary atmosphere of the studio version of 'Sitting On Top Of The World' was a fierce vitality from all three musicians which climaxed in Clapton's heroic final lick.

Of the studio tracks each member of the group had his own. Clapton's contribution, 'Badge', clearly reflected new influences and indicated a new direction. One influence was George

Harrison, who wrote the song with him and played rhythm guitar on the session (as L'Angelo Misterioso); another was the Band. For Cream the track was uncharacteristically brief at 2.45; there were, conspicuously, no solos; and the sound, with the three-piece augmented by piano and Mellotron (played by producer Felix Pappalardi), was a direct result of Clapton insisting to Bruce and Baker that the music of the Band's *Music From Big Pink* should be Cream's model. In fact, the Band's influence pervaded the other two studio tracks as well, both of which were short of four minutes and featured keyboards. 'Badge', when it was released as a single with Baker's 'What A Bringdown' in March 1969, made little impression on the charts, probably because it was so unlike conventional Cream.

Although *Goodbye* did not appear until more than three months after Cream's public adieu, it was by no means the last of the group's record releases. In October 1969 *Best Of Cream*, a compilation of tracks from earlier albums, was released and reached No. 5 in the charts in December. Then, in March 1970, following a front page story based on rumours that the group would reform for the Isle of Wight Festival later in the year, which were quickly denied by Robert Stigwood, the Stigwood Organization announced the 'discovery' of unreleased tracks in America. *Live Cream* duly appeared in June. It was, according to one reviewer, 'an invaluable collector's item – let's hope there's more to come'. True, it was a collector's item, but that was its only value, for it was a tawdry set that included only one new title, 'Lawdy Mama', which turned out virtually to be 'Strange Brew' with different words. As a placebo for the withdrawal symptoms of Cream freaks it worked wonders, enjoyed an extended chart run through the late summer, and was voted top British album in September's *Melody Maker* poll, where, of course, Clapton, Bruce and Baker were named as the world's leading exponents of their respective instruments.

Two years later, during a lull in Clapton's career, came *Live Cream Volume 2*, which included yet another version of 'Politician' but only one previously unheard cut, 'Steppin' Out'. Within a matter of weeks a *History Of Eric Clapton* appeared, a haphazard anthology that contained five tracks from Cream albums. Both were minor hits. And Cream's material was refurbished yet again in 1973 as a double album, *Heavy Cream*. What made this collection unique was the inclusion of a solitary track which had not thus far appeared on an album, but it was an expensive way to buy the group's second single, 'I Feel Free', for those who didn't have it already. Then there was *Cream* in 1975. It was basically a reissue of the group's first album, *Fresh Cream*, which had been unavailable in Britain for some time, although it had been cassetted as *Full Cream* in 1970. In addition it contained the group's first single, 'Wrapping Paper', and 'The Coffee Song', a European B-side that had not been issued in Britain. Even if Polydor and the Robert Stigwood Organization had allowed Cream to rest in peace, it is doubtful that the public would have forgotten them. Their memory would have lingered on unprompted, for Cream left an indelible taste on a great many palates. For Clapton, Bruce and Baker, however, that taste caused a nasty hangover. Whatever any of them did subsequently was inevitably compared to Cream, whenever they were interviewed the questions turned with equal inevitability to Cream, and periodically there were rumours of the group reforming.

More than a year after Cream's demise Bruce was forced to admit, 'I suppose whatever Eric, Ginger and myself do will be compared with Cream. It's very difficult really because people have got their minds made up about us.' At the time he had been touring with his own group as Jack Bruce and Friends, but was unable to shake off the ghost of Cream. 'I think the British audiences expected lots of Cream numbers,' he said defensively, 'in fact we only did three Cream songs out of a total of eighteen. Anyway the three we did do were mine in the first place. It's true, though, the audiences didn't know exactly what to expect really.' Anxious to assert his new identity, Bruce insisted his billing should not contain any reference to Cream, and actually cancelled a concert with Lifetime in October 1970 because the words 'ex-Cream' contravened the terms of the contract.

Clapton, when asked about the group in mid-1970, answered obliquely, 'I felt sort of disoriented about Cream. It didn't coincide with the way I felt about it. It was very strange. I still like a lot of the records we made, but there was something wrong somewhere. There was a weakness.' Later he became more outspoken.

Ginger Baker evidently did not mind discussing the group. In May 1971, following a spate of rumours about Cream reforming, he was unusually garrulous. Beginning with the formation of the group, he explained, 'Originally the idea was that it was to be my band, I knew it would be successful. Jack and Eric wanted it to be co-operative. I said that the writing should also be shared as I was getting nothing extra for the work I was doing [in establishing a business footing for the group]. But Jack and Eric said, "No, whoever did the writing should get the royalties." After three months I was dissatisfied with the situation ... I was informed they were getting a new drummer. Why they didn't, I don't know.

But it's just as well they didn't. The seeds of the break-up were there from the beginning. Many times I had to drink myself into a torpor before I could work with them.... Now I'm not prepared to work with any of them again under any circumstances. Two of the Cream numbers which I had a large part of the writing, I got no credits, and therefore no royalties. It wasn't just through money that Cream broke up. I did well myself, and because I've got my head screwed on I'm still okay. Recently it was put to me that it would be a good idea to get Cream together again. I said I would do it if it was done in the right way. Nothing was to be said in public until agreement was reached, but right away it was stated that Cream was to reform.' His explanation did nothing to stop the rumours. Less than two months later the pop press carried stories that he and Bruce were to play together again. But there was, as always, one piece missing from the jigsaw; on this occasion it was Clapton, holidaying in the South of France, from whom there was enigmatically 'no news'.

Along with the perks that went with being an ex-member of Cream, like a guaranteed audience for future projects and a reputation that would have seen each of them through the seventies if they'd never played another note, there were drawbacks. It was hard to live down those two and a half years together, and only Clapton succeeded completely in shaking off the spectre of Cream. While Baker blundered from one overblown band to another, Bruce fell in with Cream's army of imitators when, in 1972, he replaced the group's former record producer Felix Pappalardi in Mountain, an unexceptional heavy metal trio that survived on the bass player's name for two years as West, Bruce and Laing.

Why Cream broke up remained unexplained by theories of lost direction, role rejection or the usual musical differences. Besides, why shouldn't they have broken up? Just because they played together didn't mean they had to stay together. The final split was as straightforward as the end of a love affair. Having fulfilled themselves within their relationship, they parted. There was, quite simply, no longer any reason to be together. And no one got hurt. Did they?

Five

BLIND FAITH – CAN'T FIND MY WAY HOME

When Clapton was asked about his future plans in December 1968, shortly after Cream's farewell concert, he said he intended to produce a film in Hollywood. More relevantly he added that he wanted to form another band. 'I want to work with American musicians,' he said, 'because most of the good English musicians I know are already in groups and settled.' (This perennial problem was still on his mind years later, when he complained, 'Most people these days seem more concerned about being in the same group for good and they don't really want to entertain the idea of branching off or just spending a couple of months with someone else, because it would hurt their present job. They'd get the boot from the band they were in or it would upset somebody somewhere. I'm like it to quite a large extent too. If I'm offered the chance to go and play on someone's record, I immediately wonder what my band will think when they find out. It seems to be a prevalent attitude. You've got your actual session musicians and you've got your bands. It's a sign of old age.')

However, the same issue of *Melody Maker* that carried the interview with Clapton ran a front page report on the break-up of Traffic which led journalist Chris Welch to speculate, 'Now both Eric and Steve [Winwood] are free with the break-up of their groups, there is a strong possibility they may get a group together, or at least record.'

This was a shrewd guess, because Clapton and Winwood were known to have a deep and longstanding respect for each other which dated from the days of the Spencer Davis Group's residency at the Marquee Club, when Clapton would regularly sit in. Asked in 1966 what he thought of Clapton, Winwood had replied, 'Great guitarist, great image, and I like him very much. He influenced my playing to a certain extent, although I was more influenced by his influences. I think the Cream are fantastic. I first met him a couple of months after he left the Yardbirds, and he was with John Mayall. We used to blow together, then a lot of things happened – like pop success. He's changed a lot and developed his attitudes to music.' Apart from Thursday nights at the Marquee, one of those blows had taken place in a recording studio with an impromptu line-up that included Ben Palmer (piano), Jack Bruce (bass), the Spencer Davis Group's Pete York (drums), and Paul Jones (harmonica); Winwood sang and played organ. Three tracks appeared on an Elektra sampler, *What's Shakin'*, but they were ragged and undistinguished, as was to be expected from a group that met for one rehearsal and spent only half an hour in the studio. The sessions by the Powerhouse, as they were called on record, were evidently not the basis for the mutual admiration which existed between Clapton and Winwood.

By the end of Cream the hyperbole that had turned bands into supergroups had transformed blows and jams into supersessions. Clapton, apparently in no hurry to commit his future, was naturally invited to take part. He played at the Rolling Stones' 'Rock And Roll Circus' with John Lennon and others, which was filmed at Internal Studios in Wembley, and at an uncomfortable session at Staines, where musicians included Roland Kirk, Jack Bruce, Ron Burton, Vernon Martin, Dick Heckstall-Smith and Jon Hiseman. In this unwieldly union of jazz and rock Clapton was, perhaps, for once out of his depth; at least he hinted at difficulties when he admitted, 'It was very demanding working with Kirk. I said, "Let's do a blues then, Roland," and he said, "All right – one, two, one, two, three, four," and I've never had to play at that kind of tempo before.' In fact, he was happiest jamming privately with Steve Winwood.

Even before the New Year it was suggested that the pair would collaborate on a recording project, though neither was prepared to confirm the fact. At the beginning of January Winwood said of Clapton, 'He wants to take it easy so I'm just going to hang about and see what happens. Lots of things might come along and I want to take a trip to the States.' While Clapton insisted a few weeks later, 'As far as Stevie Winwood, Ginger Baker and myself are concerned, we are just jamming and we have no definite plans for the future.' But however reluctant they were to make definite plans, the combination of Clapton and Winwood held too much promise to be allowed to remain in so vague a form. In early April it was announced that a group comprising Clapton, Winwood and Ginger Baker would tour Scandinavia in May, followed by a British debut at a free concert in Hyde Park, London, on 7 June. Furthermore, the band had already recorded, as Clapton himself confirmed: 'We've been in the studios most of the time and done several songs – one of mine, two by Dylan, one by Buddy Holly and one by Steve. We've got enough to release two albums already. We all want to get on with it.' The new band was, he insisted, 'totally different' from Cream – 'Steve is really the focal point.'

This last piece of news was no surprise, since he had declared his aim to shed the responsibilities of front man when Cream's break-up had been announced the previous summer. The other burden he clearly wanted to rid himself of was the reluctant role of guitar god; he was more than ready to abdicate in favour of Jimi Hendrix. 'I'm very surprised I've got a reputation,' he said with unnecessary self-deprecation. 'You assume people have forgotten you, then you get a super show and get surprised at how much people expect of you. I do worry a lot about this. I don't know if my playing keeps up with my image. I do my best. I'm happy if I've got a little riff to play. I don't see myself as a great solo guitarist – that's not my bag, that's Jimi's ... I'm very aware of the pressures of reputation and image, and it's all bullshit. I think I'm good enough, which is true and false. I can only do my best.'

All in all there was little excuse for misunderstanding his intentions for the new group. It was already apparent that hardcore Cream fans would have to amend their expectations of their hero. But such was the prestige of this all-star line-up that less thought was given to its music than to its marketability. The music was simply dismissed in glorious, irrational assumptions that lent poignant irony to the group's chosen name, Blind Faith. It was the commercial potential that made the news. 'Offers for the band are already said to be topping the Cream's financial record,' revealed one report, while another, from New York, stated, 'The asking price per concert for their tour is reported to be twenty thousand dollars against percentages of each gate. This could be a multi-million-dollar tour, and the first to feature a true supergroup.' The mercenary finger in the musical pie has always aggravated Eric Clapton. It prodded him into leaving the Yardbirds back in 1965 and still inspires his loathing. 'I hate it,' he says, 'and that's why I don't like to get involved in any of the financial side of it at all, because I think it's disgusting. I know if I actually did ever have a look at the books and got interested, it would corrupt my value of the music.'

In May the group made the pop front pages again, when the addition of Family's bass guitarist Rick Grech to Blind Faith's line-up was announced. The group's debut in Hyde Park was confirmed along with a subsequent Scandinavian tour and an American tour that would start early in July. During the week which preceded the free concert the group was again the subject of cover stories in the pop press as the event was built up to mammoth proportions.

Discussion of Blind Faith's debut even reached the columns of *Melody Maker*'s letters page. 'Blind Faith fail?' wrote one prematurely committed fan. 'Someone has to be joking. It is a very good name and I feel sure that they are a success even before they produce a single recording. Almost Beatle status.' But the Reverend T. E. Winsor expressed a more critical view: 'Why all the imbecilic commotion over the new pop group called Blind Faith. It is a distressing feature of today's youth that a large proportion of them can be wrapped up in adulation over the music of a group of long-haired louts which they are yet to hear. It is a pity your readers do not bestow such Blind Faith in Our Lord as they bestow on such people.' While this letter prompted a flood of angry replies, it nonetheless contained an appropriate warning to the public's untempered anticipation. But it was either too late or simply ignored.

By nine o'clock on the morning of 7 June there were an estimated seven thousand people in the park, clustered in and around the Cockpit's natural amphitheatre; many had spent the night there. When the Third Ear Band opened the concert at half past two some estimates made the crowd as large as 150,000. The Edgar Broughton Band, Ritchie Havens and Donovan followed. Describing the event, one reporter wrote, 'There was something almost Biblical about the unique free concert given by the new supergroup and friends in London's Hyde Park on Saturday.... The spectacle of thousands of people sitting on the grass, packed tightly together and simply listening to music in silence was quite uplifting.' Maybe that's the way it seemed from the press enclosure, but out in the crowd it was a long and uncomfortable wait. Only a divine miracle would have satisfied the audience by the time Blind Faith walked on stage. Unfortunately Clapton had given up playing God.

Their set was mostly remarkable for its lack of flamboyance.It was, in short, a let down. The pop press, who had fuelled the expectations of their readers, naturally tried hard to conceal their disappointment. 'They played for over an hour,' the same reporter wrote defensively, 'tastefully, almost gently, in contrast to the violence of Cream, with arranged passages well together.... As it was it proved a warming experience to see and hear them at last united and making such a splendid gesture to their fans.' The fans, however, were less tactful. According to one, 'It was very disappointing. It seemed very much like Stevie Winwood plus a backing group – Rick Grech played too quietly,

Ginger Baker's drum solo sounded weak and aimless, while Eric Clapton seemed too content to just ride along and the lack of fire on his part contributed greatly to the group's apparent lack of imagination.' Having been built up so high, the group had a long way to fall.

'It was such a shame,' Clapton recalls. 'It started out so quietly, you know. It went for a long time, just jamming and rehearsing, before anyone knew anything about it and suddenly – BANG! We were faced with the ultimate dilemma – that we weren't ready and *they* were.' Under-rehearsed, short of material, they appeared to approach the concert as casually as if they were on the stage of a small club. Rick Grech played the new boy, anonymously; Winwood grinned a lot; Clapton attempted to merge into his Marshall stack. They could have *tried* harder, if nothing else. Only Baker broke sweat, working hard, attempting to bring the band to life and hold the set together. But then he had a reason to try harder, since he must have been aware that Winwood and Clapton would happily have let him go and brought in Jim Capaldi, Traffic's drummer and a songwriter besides, a dual role that would have been of value to a group that needed inspiration as much as horsepower. That fact only made the papers once, when the suggestion that Baker might be replaced was squashed.

Almost inevitably, public belief in the band proved more immediately durable than memory. Or perhaps Blind Faith were forgiven rather than the gig forgotten. Either way when their album, *Blind Faith*, was released in August, advance orders saw it into the charts, which it topped before the end of September.

In contrast to Cream's pyrotechnics the record fizzled as flamboyantly as a slow fuse, while its total of six tracks was skimpy enough to suggest there was more smoke than spark. Only two songs stood out – Winwood's 'Can't Find My Way Home' and Clapton's 'Presence Of The Lord' – and they were both good enough to establish themselves long term on the list for Clapton's stage set.

'Presence Of The Lord' especially was a revelation, conveying a sense of inner peace which was interrupted by a short, stunning wahwah solo. Asked the following year about the song's religious theme, Clapton explained, 'I do find songs of praise are one of my greatest inspirations. I constantly thank the Lord for being on the earth and for giving me the power to be able to play and entertain people. And now He's given me the power to sing and to communicate. I owe it to Him.'

The contented sentiments of his lyrics – 'I have finally found a way to live/Just like I never could before' – contrasted strongly with the feelings he expressed in a more conventional manner about his music around the time the song was recorded. 'I feel as if I have achieved nothing,' he said. 'I've got miles and miles to go. I have covered a lot of ground so far as material things go. They are only possessions – things to make me more materialistic. I'm trying all the time to make music that satisfies me and everybody else. That is very hard to achieve, because you can rarely make completely satisfying music.'

If Blind Faith's music was less than satisfactory, there were, for Clapton, even more disturbing adjuncts to the group's ascendancy. By the time the album was released, they were already engaged in a disastrous American tour. Clapton subsequently described it as 'very uptight', but it was much worse. At Madison Square Garden in New York there were riots, and everywhere there were disappointed audiences. 'We were playing these huge venues where we didn't have the chance to experiment,' he said, 'and it got too loud which was the very thing I was trying to avoid. If it got too quiet the audiences shouted "louder". Playing to ten thousand people is a very different situation. You lose contact with your audience. What I'd really like to do is – what we'd all like to do is play a local dance somewhere as unknowns. We were pushed to the forefront without being ready for it. On the U.S. tour we had to follow a great group on stage – Delaney and Bonnie – who deserve far more recognition. They are really a fantastic group – completely together every night ... Stevie and I before we went out to America thought – we're trapped again ... I feel the public has been cheated all along with Blind Faith because no one is as good as their hype or their promotion. It's time for groups to start giving back to their audiences what they have given to us. God knows what will happen next. I still haven't recovered from the States. I felt quite ashamed and embarrassed on that tour. It's a purely personal thing which a lot of people wouldn't understand at all. It's a battle to avoid a hype – people lay it on you that you have to use your name, and you wind up trapped in the illusion that you don't trust anybody any more because of all the promotion and all the lies – fooling everybody you've become a superstar.'

Although he wouldn't admit on his return from America that the band was finished, it was. They had indeed allowed themselves to become trapped in a vast machine which, once set in motion, would have been impossible to control even if they had known how. Which they demonstrably didn't. And the motive force behind this machine was money, not music.

The one thing Clapton salvaged from the shambles of that tour had nothing to do with Blind Faith. It was his relationship with

Delaney and Bonnie Bramlett. He had first heard them during Cream's final American tour, but it was George Harrison's enthusiasm for their music that had excited his interest sufficiently to invite them to support Blind Faith.

As he got to know Delaney and Bonnie and their musicians, he became quite infatuated with them and their music. 'I was so turned on by them I thought I could somehow try and stay in Blind Faith and skip off and do that as well. But Blind Faith didn't work like that. They wanted what I should've wanted too – a very tight integral unit – but I didn't. I was feeling quite free, so that went by the board. I don't think Stevie's ever forgiven me somehow.'

The duo's impact on Clapton is confirmed by Ben Palmer. 'Once he began to spend as much time with them as he did on the tour, his whole interest in Blind Faith evaporated almost overnight. He still observed his loyalties to the band and not for one minute did he fail to play as best he could – professionally he was not to be found wanting – but certainly another gate had opened and it was a gate into something that basically he believed in but had never really come near. Whatever else you could say about Delaney and Bonnie and some of their band, they are real people – they're certainly not rock musicians in the normal British connotation. That may sound like a harsh thing to say but I think most British rock musicians are best on stage, and that's as far as most people would ever want to take it, whereas Delaney is real to the extent that he's just as much alive whether he's got a guitar in his hands or not – and that meant an awful lot to Eric. Because they were the second band they obviously had second class treatment and he volunteered to undergo the rigours of touring for the first time in years rather than be flown to gigs ahead of them. There he was scrambling into the bus with all the enthusiasm of somebody in their first Bedford Dormobile going off to a Ricky Tick club. He enjoyed travelling again, and enjoyed being with musicians again. With Blind Faith he certainly couldn't enjoy either. In fact, we didn't see half of him except in time to go on. Travelling then had become such a disjointed affair that the whole entourage would be spread over hundreds of miles rather than everybody travel with each other – not because there was any friction or difficulty, but just because there was no point. It wasn't alive; it never lived at all.'

Whatever slim chance Blind Faith had disappeared as Clapton fell under the spell of Delaney and Bonnie's downhome charm. Back in England after the American tour he announced his intention to record a solo album, which Delaney and Bonnie

would produce. Baker, Winwood and Grech stuck together
briefly in Baker's unwieldy Airforce, until Winwood quit to
reform Traffic, which Grech was to join too. Later Winwood said
of Blind Faith. 'The group didn't last because it was four people
getting on stage and doing their own thing. Instead of one thing
being played, there were four things going on. It was an exhaust-
ing experience and it was sad that it petered out the way it did.'

At the very time *Blind Faith* was at the top of the album charts
and the group was voted Britain's Brightest Hope, Blind Faith
had virtually ceased to exist. Whatever criticisms were levelled
at the group, it must be admitted that they never had much of a
chance to prove themselves. They were suffocated by the unreasonable expectations of their audience, the cupidity of the music
industry, and their own inability to cope with either. But if the
experience left Eric Clapton any the wiser, it wasn't obvious.

Six

DELANEY AND BONNIE
– *AND* FRIENDS

Clapton's first public appearance after returning from Blind
Faith's American tour was as a member of the Plastic Ono Band
when John Lennon phoned to ask him to join the line-up for the
Toronto Rock And Roll Revival. Clapton flew out the next day.
The band – Lennon, Clapton, Klaus Voorman, Alan White, Yoko
Ono – headlined a bill that included Bo Diddley, Jerry Lee Lewis,
Chuck Berry and Little Richard. They played rock 'n' roll oldies
for half an hour before Yoko joined in. Her extraordinary perform-
ance was not what the crowd wanted. 'A few people started to
boo,' Clapton said afterwards, 'but it turned into howling along
with Yoko. Yoko has the same effect on people as a high-pitched
whistle has on a dog. Her voice is spine-chilling. Very weird ...
John and I played some feed-back guitar while she was singing.'
He subsequently played on the Plastic Ono Band's single, 'Cold
Turkey', with Lennon, Voorman and Ringo Starr, and appeared
with the band again at a UNICEF charity concert at the Lyceum
in London in December.

He also took part in some abortive recording sessions at
London's Olympic Studios with a line-up of musicians that
included George Harrison, Rick Grech, Denny Laine and Trevor
Burton. But he had already made up his mind what he wanted to
do: play lead guitar with Delaney and Bonnie and Friends.

Already attracted to Delaney and Bonnie Bramlett as people
as much as to their music, Clapton also saw in their band the
opportunity to adopt the kind of supporting role he had sought
(but failed to find) in Blind Faith. And their comparative anonymity favoured the success of his ambitions. In fact, he wasn't the
only musician searching for a stance outside the spotlight:
George Harrison and Dave Mason were equally impressed by the
low-key, freewheeling set-up. Clapton said at the time, 'I suppose
it was just a natural progression from meeting them on the Blind
Faith tour. You know, jamming with them, hanging out with
them and digging them, and really loving them as people. It's

such a change when somebody comes along who is really humble
like Delaney and Bonnie and their friends. They're willing to
work and, because there are so many of them, to work for very
little money.' But if he hoped that their obscurity would allow
him to shake off the burden of stardom, he was reckoning
without his own reputation.

His intention was to bring them to England for a tour of small
venues, but, having allowed the arrangements to be taken out of
his hands, he was unable to prevent the exploitation of his name
or the mapping out of a big-time itinerary. Worse, as the music-
business publicity machinery gathered its own relentless
momentum, he saw his new friends in whom he had placed so
much faith rapidly metamorphose into stereotype stars. The
patronage of rock royalty like Eric Clapton and George Harrison
had gone to their heads.

The effects of their sudden elevation to stardom would have
worn off in time. Delaney and Bonnie had been paying dues too
long to allow success to change them permanently. But they
didn't recover soon enough. Their disillusioned 'friends' – Bobby
Keys (saxophone), Jim Price (trumpet and trombone), Bobby
Whitlock (organ), Carl Radle (bass), Jim Gordon (drums), and
Rita Coolidge (vocals) – departed, all but Whitlock answering
their ex-colleague Leon Russell's call to join Joe Cocker for the
Mad Dogs and Englishmen tour which crisscrossed America
from March to May in 1970. And the blow to Clapton's ideals was
heavy. According to Ben Palmer, 'It was very unhappy that Eric
had placed so much confidence and trust in them very quickly at
that particular time. If he'd known them a little longer, he
would've waited and understood that this was something they
would've adjusted to, but he was totally committed to them in
every way. He was prepared to spend the rest of his life literally
with the two of them, doing whatever they thought they'd like to
do: Stigwood and Atlantic and all those people could wait until
he'd decided, and take it or leave it. He was utterly and totally
committed to them, and when suddenly they quite naturally
needed some time, I know he was shocked and hurt and he
retreated from it very quickly. They went back to America and
then all the recriminations started, like who pays for this and
who pays for that, and *he* said *he'd* pay. Just all this stuff.
Musicians don't want to hear about all that, but Eric had to hear
about a lot of it because it was all his money in the tour, so he
had to be aware of some of it and he just retreated. For weeks
after Delaney and Bonnie just weren't mentioned.'

What survived from Clapton's relationship with Delaney and
Bonnie was a live album, *Delaney And Bonnie And Friends On*

Tour With Eric Clapton, which revealed the limitations of their particular brand of blue-eyed soul as much as its appeal. And there was Clapton's first solo album.

When the project of an album produced by the Bramletts had first been made public in the autumn of 1969, Clapton said he wanted to record a tribute to Buddy Holly. Blind Faith had reworked 'Well All Right', but now he was insisting, 'I want to do a lot of Buddy Holly songs that perhaps people haven't heard before – lots of old B-sides that used to knock me out like "Fool's Paradise" ... I think I'll call my album "Buddy's B-Sides".' However serious his intentions were, they didn't survive the trip to America, where *Eric Clapton* was recorded. The sessions took place in Los Angeles with a studio band comprised of Delaney and Bonnie and Friends with the addition of Leon Russell on piano. Not surprisingly, the album reflected their influence both in its sound and its style.

The mixture was too strong for the British public, who had reacted badly to Clapton's quest for anonymity, and the record was his first since he left the Yardbirds not to make the top ten. It didn't please the critics either. *Melody Maker*'s reviewer wrote, 'What is surprising, and most disappointing, is the extent to which Eric has submerged himself in the Delaney and Bonnie sound to the point where it really does become a Delaney and Bonnie album featuring E. Clapton (guitar).... Obviously it's not a BAD album, but what's sad is that it lacks any real Clapton identity. Eric has meant so much to British pop that it is invidious to knock him now for doing something that he enjoys. But let's hope that he regains a sense of identity, purpose and direction, and realizes that musically he really doesn't need the Delaney and Bonnie Show.' Despite his understandable pride in the album, Clapton himself was evidently worried about the way it would be received. Shortly before its release he said, 'You never know how records will sell. I listen to the album and I like it but I don't know why I do. And I can't fit it into any special category of music that I've heard before, so I'm a little worried that people may have trouble recognizing it and may reject it.... The thing is that I got so much help on this album that I couldn't let anybody down. I just had to do it. It wasn't a question of proving anything to anybody. I had to do it. The love that went around among everybody involved on the record was just so powerful. I'm really proud of it. I love the sound of the whole thing and I never thought that would be possible.'

In fact, Clapton's fans' prejudice against Delaney and Bonnie, whom they clearly regarded as his Delilah, made them deaf to the album's unquestionable qualities. Discounting a couple of jams, it contained some lively Clapton/Bramlett collaborations, a sympathetic version of the then unknown J. J. Cale's 'After Midnight', and Leon Russell's rousing anthem 'Blues Power'. And if his guitar playing was understated, his singing was unexpectedly confident throughout.

As if this new concentration on songwriting and singing was not sufficiently self-evident from the record, he outlined his ambitions elsewhere. 'I don't think guitar playing is enough,' he said. 'It's very hard for me to see why anyone would laud a cat who just plays the guitar. It's really not enough somehow. If I was a great songwriter or a great singer, then I wouldn't be so humble about it. I wouldn't be so shy. Until I am either a great songwriter or a great singer, then I shall carry on being embarrassed when people come on with the praise.' *Eric Clapton* certainly didn't go all the way, but it was a giant stride in the right direction. (The sessions also brought the unexpected bonus of a blow with King Curtis, which resulted in the saxophonist's instrumental single, 'Teasin''. According to Clapton, 'Curtis just came up with this line – "let's play this together" – and we played it together, and then Delaney had a little thing, and it was constructed in about half an hour. If it comes down to it, what I would really like to have been is a saxophone player. I play guitar in terms of what a good saxophone player like Curtis or Junior Walker plays – long, screeching, beautiful notes. So being able to play the same lines with him was a mind-blower.')

The loosest numbers were the two openers. The instrumental 'Slunky' on the first side simply evolved in the studio when Leon Russell arrived one day, and 'Bottle Of Red Wine' on side two, which Clapton dismissed as 'just a shuffle', was composed on the way to a session. Both, though, established the album's buoyant mood. Even where the content of the songs was not optimistic, as on 'Don't Know Why', the feeling persisted that the musicians were all enjoying themselves.

Several of the Bramlett/Clapton compositions grew out of earlier ideas of Bramlett's which were tidied up and adapted to suit Clapton's voice. They were all, unquestionably, *songs* – well constructed and economically performed; the longest track on the album (and one of Clapton's perennial favourites), 'Let It Rain', even extended by the nearest thing to a characteristic Clapton solo present, lasted only a little over five minutes. The one exception to the album's overall mood was his own love song, 'Easy Now', performed with just an acoustic guitar and double-tracked harmonies. Its content anticipated his imminent obsession with love themes.

Clapton's singing, which had not been heard since Cream, and

then infrequently, echoed his playing in its avoidance of osten-
tation, but it was sufficiently expressive to make the listener
wonder why he had allowed Jack Bruce to monopolize the
microphone as much as he had. (He once explained it this way: 'I
was very shy, Jack was very pushy – a combination of the two.
Actually he was shy too. He was pushed into it by me and
Ginger, because Ginger wasn't going to sing and I didn't have
any experience at it and Jack obviously did.') This new-found
vocal confidence was down to Delaney and dated from Blind
Faith's US tour. 'Delaney sort of sowed the seed with me when he
told me that I should be using my voice, because people wanted
me to sing, and I firmly believed him. Whether he was deliberately trying to pull me out of the group or what, that was the way
he went about it. He said, "They want to hear you play and hear
you sing – you should be out there with your own band."'

Clapton also credits Delaney Bramlett for introducing him to
the music of J. J. Cale, an abiding influence ever since. 'He
turned me on to "After Midnight",' he recalls. 'He said someone
should cover it, and if I didn't, he would. So we did it. He actually
did a version with the same track – with his voice instead of mine
– and we argued about it and he gave in.' Released as a single, it
made the US top twenty towards the end of 1970.

Perhaps the key song on the album was 'Blues Power', written
apparently for him by Leon Russell. 'It feels like he wrote it for
me,' Clapton confirmed. 'I don't want to be pretentious and say
he did, but it's easy to sing and it's exactly what I wanted to say.'
Its words neatly expressed his self-assurance and happiness in
his music: 'I knew all the time, but now I'm going to let you
know/I'm gonna keep on rockin' no matter if it's fast or slow/
Ain't gonna stop until the twenty-fifth hour/Cos now I'm living
on blues power' or, in another verse, 'There ain't no need for me
to be a wall flower/Cos now I'm living on blues power.'

A careless collector of his own output, Clapton ended up
without a copy of his first solo album and didn't hear it again
until an interviewer arrived at his house in 1974 with a bag of
records for reference. 'I conned them all off him,' he recalls,
'because I didn't have any, and that one knocked me out because
I hadn't heard it in years. Apart from my vocal being very fresh
and young and sort of small sounding, I thought the groove was
unbelievable – the *band!*'

As he had done before, by the time the album was released in
August 1970 Clapton had moved on. In mid-May a spokesman for
the Robert Stigwood Organization had stated, 'Eric is not
forming a group.' A week later it was announced that Clapton
would play at a charity concert for Dr Spock's Civil Liberties

Legal Defence Fund for anti-war protesters at London's Lyceum on 14 June with a group formed from Delaney and Bonnie's 'friends' who were due to fly into Britain that week. Even before the Lyceum concert had taken place, Clapton decided to keep the band together. He named his musicians the Dominos. And Eric? He was Derek.

Since completing his solo album he had taken part in a number of sessions, playing on recordings by Howlin' Wolf, Doris Troy and George Harrison, but his desire to sing had been unfulfilled. Hence his reincarnation as Derek.

As they appeared at the Lyceum, the Dominos were: Bobby Whitlock (organ), Carl Radle (bass), Jim Gordon (drums) and Dave Mason (guitar). Their performance was greeted with the kind of mixed reaction that by then must have been familiar to Clapton. Chris Welch wrote in *Melody Maker*, 'Eric's band seemed well together, with Dave Mason on second guitar, and American friends making a good rhythm section. The numbers tended to be those effective two-chord riffs that Delaney and Bonnie feature, medium blues and several unrecognizable songs. Eric sang a lot, looked confident and cheerful, smiled and chatted easily. When he finally switched to electric guitar, a great cheer went up. There were also demands for the organ to turn down, as it was tending to drown everything. Then it was possible to hear some nice playing in a country style, and there was more than a flash of the old blues magic. There were no fireworks, but the band radiated peace. "Do you want me to turn up?' asked Eric, and the children said, "Yes".' Some fans felt differently, though. According to one, 'Unless Eric Clapton finds his feet again as a good, fast and tasteful guitar player, the critics will find another good guitarist to praise. If Clapton wants to lose his crown to another young guitarist, he only has to carry on with what he's doing.' While another complained, 'After seeing Eric Clapton at London's Lyceum, looking like a degreased Elvis Presley and playing poorly disguised rock and roll, I came away feeling bored, bewildered and thoroughly sick. Sick of the people who cheer the name – and not the music.'

Clapton confined himself to reassuring his fans that the group would 'be getting more into blues' on the club dates that would follow a month's writing and rehearsing, but Dave Mason was less reticent. 'Eric has come out much stronger,' he said. 'He's really singing now, and writing some very pretty songs. He's getting himself together now; he's been put where he is, and he's starting something new. It's very valuable for me too – I haven't played with a group for ages, and it's good to get back. My playing isn't as good as I want, nothing like Eric's of course, but being in the band will enable me to get it together again because things come much faster when you're playing in a group. Having watched the Blind Faith go down, I know that this trip has got to be handled right. All I'm really interested in is making music with people.' In Derek and the Dominos he saw the possibilities 'for each of us to do our own things, and to find out new things together.... If we could do that it will be beautiful, but I want to retain my own thing, my own identity, too, because that's very important to me.' Ironically, when Derek and the Dominos reappeared in public, Mason was missing from the line-up.

The group played club and ballroom dates in England before flying to Miami in September in order to record an album at Criteria Recording Studios.

They had already recorded with Phil Spector, and 'Tell The Truth' had been scheduled for release early in October, but the single was withdrawn at the last moment because of the group's 'increasing dissatisfaction with the record' and 'After Midnight' was hurriedly released in its place. The reason for its withdrawal was that a new version, recorded in Miami for inclusion on Derek and the Dominos' album, was so much better that the group didn't want anyone to hear the original.

Although disappointing for those who were anxious to hear Clapton's new band on record, this was good news from the sessions at Criteria Studios and in retrospect an entirely understandable decision, for the resulting double album, *Layla And Other Assorted Love Songs*, ranks among Clapton's greatest achievements.

The success of the project can perhaps be most easily attributed to those catch-alls of chemistry and coincidence. On the album's four sides everything came together with an extraordinary unity, a unity that has seldom been attained in rock and certainly had not in Clapton's own career. His songs, his playing, his singing, his musicians, the production: all these elements combined in that recording studio at that moment in time.

The single-minded inspiration behind his songs created the nearest thing to a 'concept' album Clapton has ever executed. The throwaway reference in its title to 'assorted love songs' was intended more seriously than it sounded, for Clapton's inspiration throughout was unrequited love. He later explained to a *Rolling Stone* reporter, 'It was actually about an emotional experience, a woman that I felt really deeply about and who turned me down, and I had to kind of pour it out in some way.... It was the heaviest thing going on at the time ... I didn't consciously do it, though, it just happened that way. That was what I wanted to write about most of all.' The woman in question was George Harrison's wife Patti, who later left Harrison for Clapton, and whom Clapton eventually married in 1979; at the time, however, she rejected him. According to Clapton, Harrison had once 'grabbed one of my chicks and so I thought I'd get even with him one day, on a petty level, and it grew from that, you know. She was trying to attract his attention, trying to make him jealous, and so she used me, you see, and I fell madly in love with her.'

A one-sided love affair might have played havoc with Clapton's heart, but on the evidence of the eight songs he came up with on *Layla*, there was compensation in a hefty creative kick. For five of them he collaborated with Bobby Whitlock, as he did just once, but crucially, with Jim Gordon, the spark to ignite the title track, while the remaining six songs – Jimi Hendrix's poignant 'Little Wing' and a handful of blues – matched the mood of the loser in love.

By the time of the *Layla* sessions Derek and the Dominos had reached that beautiful balance between freshness and familiarity. And there was a telling addition to the line-up in Duane Allman, a Southern slide guitarist who had first grabbed Clapton's attention with his playing on Wilson Pickett's 'Hey Jude'. (According to Clapton, 'It scared the pants off me – it really did.') Atlantic Records' producer Tom Dowd knew Allman's work well from company sessions at Rick Hall's Fame studios in Muscle Shoals, Alabama, where 'Hey Jude' had been recorded, and through Atlantic's involvement with the Allman Brothers Band, and he was well acquainted with Clapton, having engineered Cream's sessions in New York. As executive producer of *Layla* he made it his business to bring the two guitarists together.

'Working with them both I thought they had a great deal in common,' he explained later. 'Eric had a healthy respect for what he heard Duane do, while Duane, listening to a Cream LP, would say, "Man, I wish I could play like that dude in Cream." They were almost identical in personality, strong people, but very soft spoken. Neither of them was loud or raucous, but when it came to doing something they'd pick up their instrument with authority. The chemistry was there. They could look at each other and know what was going down.'

That chemistry brought the best out of Clapton. And he knew it. 'It was so invigorating to meet someone who didn't subscribe to any other guitarist's style of playing. *That* was it, *that* was the only one you were ever going to hear play like that. So you could just do your own thing and stay yourself, and it would just blend – it was amazing!' However extended the interplay of their guitars, Clapton and Allman never lost direction, and some of their duets were literally unforgettable.

The title track is one of rock's timeless classics. Although 'Layla' flopped unaccountably when first released as a single, it made the top ten on both sides of the Atlantic as a reissue in 1972 and did even better in the UK a decade later when it reached No. 4 in April 1982. And it has dominated every live set Clapton's played since.

Tom Dowd's testimony is impressive. 'I said when I finished making *Layla*, "That is the best album I've made in ten years," and the album I was referring to that I thought was another incredible album that I'd been involved with was the first Ray Charles *Genius* album, where we used Count Basie's orchestra and so forth and his own band, and I thought that was an album that would live for ever. And I said it about *Layla*. *Layla* came out and was not successful the first year. It was after the second year that it came out that all of a sudden everybody said "Wow!" But the first year wasn't that successful and I was disappointed, because the feeling on it and the feeling I had when we were doing it and when it was all done was: "This is it, this is a masterpiece, this is a gem – nothing will touch it." It was a classic.'

(Dowd also recounts an amusing incident when he was producing Lynyrd Skynyrd some years later. Invited to keyboard player Billy Powell's house, he was introduced to Powell's daughter Layla, so named because when he and his wife had fallen in love the album was on the turntable. Dowd inquired what would have happened if the baby had been a boy. It turned out that Powell's wife's sister had had a boy around the same time. His name was Derek.)

The song has dominated every live set Clapton has played since. 'Through all the numbers,' he said in 1975, 'you'd get "Layla! Layla!", you just couldn't get a word in edgewise when I'd introduce the band. You couldn't even *play*, they were just shouting, letting off firecrackers and God knows what until they got what they wanted. So we decided to get it out of the way and just carry on – satisfy them right at the beginning and maybe they'll accept what we give them.'

But 'Layla' was always more than a crowd pleaser. Its lyrics explained the source of the album's inspiration:

> *I tried to give you consolation*
> *When your old man let you down*
> *Like a fool I fell in love with you*
> *You turned my whole world upside down*
>
> *Layla, you've got me on my knees*
> *Layla, I'm begging, darling, please*
> *Layla darling, won't you ease my worried mind*

Let's make the best of the situation
Before I finally go insane
Please don't say I'll never find a way
Or tell me all my love's in vain

Ironically, the significance of the words was all but submerged in a musical tidal wave which broke around the listener's ears from the opening riff through to the calm of the closing passage, and Duane Allman's slide work in the central guitar section turned every superlative into an understatement. Soar? It raked the stratosphere.

Clapton and Allman didn't record together again. Postponed by Clapton's withdrawal into his own private world, a renewal of their partnership was put off permanently when Allman was killed on his motorcycle in October 1971. (The Dominos were touched again by tragedy when Carl Radle died of a drug overdose in 1980 and more bizarrely four years later when Jim Gordon was found guilty of the brutal murder of his mother.)

In the light of Clapton's treatment by the music press since Cream broke up, it was predictable that *Layla* would be received less than ecstatically. One reviewer described it as 'a double album of songs that ranged from the magnificent to a few lengths of complete boredom', adding that although it was 'certainly far more musical than his last album' there were 'again some inexcusable portions'. What was less easy to understand, however, was its commercial failure. As Clapton put it years later, '*Layla* ... died a death, but, as far as I was concerned, I'd've put that album up against anybody's that was out at the time.'

It's hard to believe that Clapton's British fans were so confused by his pseudonym that they failed to recognize their former hero, but the alternative explanation – that they heard the record and rejected it – is at least as implausible. Whatever the specific cause, *Layla*'s lack of success stopped Clapton in his tracks and precipitated a long period of withdrawal.

Already the group's tour of the States through October and November had undermined much of the confidence he had held in Derek and the Dominos. In contrast to the generally unambitious venues where they had played their British dates, the American tour was scheduled for stadiums despite Clapton's reluctance, in Jim Gordon's words, 'to do the superstar routine'. Others shared his discontent. One American reporter wrote, 'It's time for Eric Clapton to re-evaluate his position in rock and roll. Two double concerts at the Santa Monica Civic Auditorium and the Pasadena Auditorium for Derek and the Dominos left more to be desired than any concert in recent memory. Possibly the problem was aggravated by the fact that the musicianship is so fine; what else would anyone expect. Yet the evenings were boring, plagued by loud sound and muddled singing. The audience was absolutely no help either. Many walked out during the performances and those that stayed seemed bent upon calling out Clapton's name during his solos. The sold-out houses that were hoped for during this Clapton tour never materialized; in fact many shows were less than half-filled. It's time the Stigwood Organization stopped shoving Clapton into positions that he cannot, and possibly does not want to fill.'

Less than three months later, in February 1971, Clapton announced his temporary retirement from live performance. 'That doesn't mean I shall not be playing in public again,' he said, 'but I need to take stock of my life and see which direction I ought to go.'

At that stage he still planned to keep the Dominos together, and as long as he did the hope remained that he would continue to record. Then, in May during a recording session in a London studio, Derek and the Dominos broke up. Clapton said later, 'Once I'd got *Layla* out of my system, I didn't want to do any more with the Dominos. I didn't want to play another note.' At the time of the split the group were supposedly recording a second album, but no new studio tracks were issued.

Although both single and album versions of his authentic labour of love made the British and American charts in 1972, this vindication came too late to save Clapton from his self-imposed exile. In 1973 a set of live recordings was issued as *Derek & The Dominos In Concert*: nine cuts spread over four sides. It wasn't until 1974, almost four years after the release of *Layla*, that he returned to the recording studio. In the meantime he might as well have been dead.

Seven

THE GUITAR HERO
AS JUNKIE

On 1 August 1971 Eric Clapton played two shows with George Harrison at Madison Square Garden, New York, in aid of the refugee children of Bangla Desh; on 11 December 1971 he made an unexpected and unobtrusive appearance at the Rainbow Theatre, London, with Leon Russell; on 13 January 1973 he turned out for two performances at the Rainbow with a backing group led by Pete Townshend. The rest of the time for more than three years he mostly concerned himself with dope. There were no records save for the inevitable, interminable repackaging of old tracks, and no interviews. That's not a lot of output for the world's number one guitarist, but it's an awful lot of H.

Clapton may not have been the first junkie in rock and roll, but he was one of the luckiest. He came out on the other side.

Although drugs and music have been close, if uneasy companions for a long while, the hard stuff had by tradition been associated specifically with the jazz world. While the Beatles were popularizing marijuana and acid, and Pete Townshend was owning up that the Who were pillheads, the junkies were shooting up in secret. Even in late 1966 Jonathan King's suggestion that the use of pot (sic) was widespread among pop musicians had brought about indignant and immediate denials. Clapton himself had been asked to comment. 'I really have no idea how prevalent it is,' he said. 'If people do smoke I suppose it's to be hip – because that's what most people are striving to be. Morally I don't think there's much harm, but I don't think it would do your health much good. I suppose it's really up to the individual.'

With more poignant irony his manager had commented on the same subject in 1970. 'What I'd hate to see,' said Robert Stigwood, 'is the music industry becoming synonymous with drug taking and that sort of thing. The majority of people in the business have nothing to do with drugs. It's the minority that give everybody a bad name through their behaviour.' Clapton was already riding the down spiral.

What finally sank him was *Layla*: the private emotional tur-moil that inspired it and the public apathy that greeted it. He simply shut himself away in the Surrey countryside and did drugs. For three years he felt little but the need to score more. It was an expensive habit. It cost him much of the money he'd made, cost him his health, almost robbed him of his career and in the end, maybe, would have cost him his life.

He nearly didn't appear at the Bangla Desh Concert. He was sick, too sick to attend the rehearsals at Nola Studios on West 57th Street, and Jesse Ed Davis was brought in to play second lead to Harrison. He didn't even make the final run through at Madison Square Garden the night before the concert, but managed to turn up in time for the first show. He played better than he should have under those circumstances, especially as he later admitted that 'just being in tune was enough of a problem for me'. Then he disappeared again.

His arrival at Leon Russell's concert at the Rainbow Theatre in London was even more unexpected. According to one of the roadies, 'He just walked on after the first number and played away.' Few members of the audience were aware of his presence and Carl Radle, who was playing with Russell's Shelter People, was surprised by the appearance of the Dominos' former leader. Afterwards Clapton retreated once more.

When he emerged for a third time from seclusion, his motives were scarcely more clearly defined. If he took part in the Bangla Desh concert because George had asked him to and sat in with the Shelter People to look up some old friends, his appearance at the Rainbow in January 1973 was more because Pete Townshend pushed him into it than because he was ready to make the comeback his fans hoped for. As he admitted to the audience at the end of the second show on Saturday 13 January, when he asked them to thank Townshend, 'I wouldn't have done it without him.'

When it was first announced in *Melody Maker* ten days before that Townshend 'had formed an instant supergroup' to back Clapton, the news was greeted with as much scepticism as excitement. The eagerness with which such an assembly of star-studded talent would have been anticipated a few years before had been tempered by disappointment. It was no longer enough just to *see* rock's heroes standing together on a stage; their music had to make it, too. The line-up reported in the same paper – Steve Winwood (keyboards), Ron Wood (bass), and Jim Keltner (drums) – did not dispel the doubts, since only Winwood had played much with Clapton before; and none had worked with any of the others. Townshend, however, was equally anxious that Clapton's comeback should be successful, and even before the news hit the streets Clapton was rehearsing with the band at Ron Wood's house on Richmond Hill.

Already the personnel had changed: Rick Grech had taken over from Wood as bass guitarist, freeing Wood to play second lead behind Clapton, and J. J. Cale's drummer, Jimmy Karstein, had replaced Keltner. Winwood's partner from Traffic, Jim Capaldi, added a second drum kit as well as helping out on vocals. Rehearsals took place every night, lasting sometimes until the following morning, until on the Wednesday before the concert the band moved out of Wood's house onto the stage of Guildford Civic Hall.

The rehearsal that day was planned to begin at five o'clock, but only Grech was remotely punctual, and the rest of the band, followed by Clapton, did not arrive until two hours later. Tuning up and jamming delayed the start still further and it was eight o'clock before they ran through the first number, 'Let It Rain'.

Up to that moment they had done nothing to send the solitary intruder at the back of the hall home for his autograph book; they certainly didn't look very special, hadn't dressed up to rehearse. Apart from their impressive battery of equipment, they could have been anybody. Rick Grech even invented an anonymous identity, the Palpitations, a name not unconnected with the effect of amyl nitrite.

But as soon as the band pulled together into 'Let It Rain', the classic Bramlett/Clapton song that had closed Clapton's solo album, a couple of things were immediately apparent. They hadn't wasted those long nights at the Wick and, what's more, Townshend's choice of personnel hadn't been haphazard. Karstein's drumming was solid but, in the American manner, not heavy-handed; Grech was sympathetic, unobtrusive, leaving spaces yet no holes; like a good actor, Winwood instilled his own personality into his supporting role without upstaging the star; Wood was getting ready to make people sit up on the night and wonder why they hadn't taken him seriously before; Townshend, confining himself rigidly to rhythm guitar, chopped that rhythm with passion and precision; only Capaldi seemed unsure of his role, as he shambled about the stage with a cowbell or a tambourine, sang alongside Clapton, but rarely sat down with a kit – the following night his drums were set up alongside Karstein's. Surrounded by his friends, Clapton glowed with genuine happiness and unreal health.

'Let It Rain' was an emphatic expression of the band's capabilities, and the sight and sound of Clapton, Townshend, Wood and Winwood singing the chorus in harmony were as enjoyable as the song itself. In addition to 'Let It Rain', the inclusion of three more songs – 'After Midnight', 'Blues Power' and 'Bottle Of Red Wine', though this was dropped from the final running order – from *Eric Clapton* showed that Clapton estimated his solo album differently from those fans who'd blacked it because of the Bramletts. Paradoxically only two numbers from Cream's repertoire were included: 'Crossroads', as the inevitable Robert Johnson homage, and the song which had signalled the end of the group, 'Badge'. Apart from Blind Faith's 'Presence Of The Lord' and Traffic's 'Pearly Queen', both of which were sung by Winwood, the remainder of the material was Derek and the Dominos': 'Roll It Over', which subsequently appeared on the *In Concert* album, and a selection of songs from *Layla* that included 'Tell The Truth', 'Why Does Love Got To Be So Sad?', 'Bell Bottom Blues', 'It's Too Late', 'Nobody Knows You When You're Down And Out', 'Key To The Highway', 'Little Wing' and, of course, 'Layla'.

By Thursday night the set was familiar enough to tempt an even later start and a series of stops for the musicians to watch themselves on video and even to tune the monitor to *Monty Python*. But Townshend was impatient to perfect the performance and wary too of the hypnotic hold TV had on Clapton, and after one interruption he called peevishly for a run-through of 'Roll It BLOODY Over'.

On Friday the equipment was moved into the Rainbow, but that night no one could be bothered to rehearse. The band performed four numbers – 'Nobody Knows You When You're Down And Out', marred by a faulty mike, 'Little Wing', 'Pearly Queen' and 'Roll It Over' – and worked out a running order. As Clapton told the band, 'I think it's been okay for days. We could've cancelled this and been all right.' They jammed (Clapton on drums, Capaldi on piano) and added the African percussionist Rebop to the line-up. Ronnie Lane's brand new mobile studio was parked behind the theatre to record both shows the following night.

When the Average White Band, playing their first big gig since coming down from Scotland, went on stage at five thirty for the first house Clapton's band were already in the dressing room. Clapton himself was missing. Backstage the atmosphere grew uncomfortably tense. He had woken up that morning convinced that he'd lost his voice. He was by that stage considerably more nervous than he had appeared to be during rehearsals and it suddenly seemed quite possible that he might not turn up for his own show. On several faces the relief was undisguised when he arrived.

During the first house there were signs of nervousness in taut vocal chords and an occasional hesitant instrument, but the audience showed no sign of disappointment and the show ran over when Clapton and his band were called back for an encore. The interval was chaotic. Outside the crowds were trying to get in for the second show, before the first audience was out, and there were hundreds without tickets waiting hopelessly for some chance of admission. And inside the backstage area was filled with the famous in spite of security so tight that Clapton's own invited guests had had to wait to get in.

By the second show the pressurized atmosphere on stage had eased, although the excitement in the audience was even more intense. The band was relaxed, the playing tight. On 'Little Wing' Ron Wood's guitar duet with Clapton was quite stunning. The set was even longer than the first had been, and by the time 'Layla' had been repeated as an encore, the band's entire rehearsed repertoire had been exhausted. Clapton thanked Townshend and it was over. Despite the continued demands for more, there was nothing more to give.

The concert could not have offered more encouragement for Clapton's rehabilitation. No one had called for 'Sunshine Of Your Love' or 'Spoonful'; no one had wondered where Bruce or Baker were; his favourite songs, his *own* songs had been unquestioningly and ecstatically received; his friends had helped him up and he'd shown them that, once standing, he could keep his feet; he'd proved to the public that he was alive, that he was still the finest guitarist in rock and roll, and more: a singer and songwriter besides. It was unthinkable that another eighteen months could pass, as they had since the Concert for Bangla Desh, before Clapton would appear in public again. But whatever he'd proved to his fellow musicians and his fans, he hadn't to himself. And why not? 'Because I was still heavily into that dope deal,' he explains flatly, 'and that's all, that was it. That's the prime reason for my negative attitude. For me it was a great thing to do, but I wasn't really there – not like the others were, it's probably a greater memory for them than it is for me. It was a very casual deal, almost like playing my own benefit. I felt the other chaps could carry the load and I'd just walk on and do what I could do. I did it purely for the fun of it – though, come to think of it, we did work fucking hard – and a great deal of gratitude is due to the chaps for getting me out of the pit I was in. It was really good of them. But I think I vanished again straight afterwards.

'It was Pete's baby really, he was the one that was hammering on my head all the time, but Pete – God bless his heart – didn't really tackle the cause, he was tackling the effect. All the time during the rehearsals and the gigs and for I don't know how long afterwards, I was still going through a really strong habit. And Pete actually overlooked that, he turned a blind eye and thought, "If we can get him on stage, maybe the power of being on stage – the *magic* – will make him think." Which it didn't obviously, because I was in cuckoo land – and I think that's why it happened that way.'

Within a matter of months it was no more than a memory to anyone: a memory that was barely revived by the release late in the year of six cuts from the shows as *Eric Clapton's Rainbow Concert*. The selection was puzzling – for instance, there was no 'Let It Rain', a stand-out on the night – and the sound was undistinguished. According to Clapton, 'I didn't want anything to do with it. Weeks later, when there was time to look at it in retrospect, it wasn't – any of it – really good quality. And in fact I had to overdub on some of them, so some of that stuff isn't genuinely live at all, and needless to say I didn't really want the album out.' Certainly it would have made a poor epitaph if he'd never returned.

Eight

THE RETURN OF THE RELUCTANT HERO

It was more than a year before the real comeback, when, detoxified by a course of electro-acupuncture, strengthened by a stay on a farm in Wales run by the brother of an ex-girlfriend, and, most importantly, totally determined to turn his back on heroin for ever, he held a guitar in his hands and found it as familiar as an old friend, then sang and enjoyed the voice he heard. Back in London, he told his manager to hire a studio and Tom Dowd as producer. He was ready to return. Robert Stigwood was sufficiently confident he was cured to invite the press to a reception in a Chinese restaurant in Soho on 10 April 1974, and there sat Clapton, cropped and alert, chatting cheerfully to Pete Townshend and Elton John. Then, having cabled Carl Radle, Clapton flew to Miami, where Stigwood had booked time at Criteria, the studios *Layla* had been recorded at four years before.

Clapton was keen to get started as soon as he arrived, and couldn't wait for Radle to turn up from Tulsa. 'I was excited, keyed up, frightened, and very pent up,' he recalls. 'There was a lot of energy going there – ready to burst out. There was time, the studio was open, it was either that or sit in the hotel room, so we went in and used whoever was about.' Into that category came George Terry, a guitarist he'd first met during the *Layla* sessions, and Yvonne Elliman, a singer whose role as Mary Magdalene in *Jesus Christ Superstar* had brought her an American hit in 1971 with 'I Don't Know How To Love Him', but whose presence at the studio had more to do with her husband Bill Oakes' role as president of Clapton's record company, RSO. By the time Radle showed up with Dick Sims (keyboards) and Jamie Oldaker (drums), both from Bob Seger's backing band, the bass guitarist's notion of a close-knit quartet – a second Derek and the Dominos – was several days out of date, and the Tulsa team were miffed initially at having to adapt to a six-piece line-up.

This uncertain start apart, the three weeks of sessions went smoothly, and were remarkably productive considering Clapton's own lack of preparation. Before he walked into Criteria he only had two songs in his head. The rest emerged in the studio. 'What we'd do is we'd walk in and jam,' he explained later, 'and then we'd listen to it back and write the song. You know, pick out a riff or part of the jam that was good, and then write a song with it. We really got it going in the end.' The band also played around with other people's songs – 'songs that I've always liked and that creep back into my memory. I just wanted to get them off my chest.'

This casual process was monitored by Tom Dowd. 'Eric is an inspirational person,' he points out, 'and when he does want to go in the studio there cannot be too much discipline and preparation because it will take away from the spontaneity, which is Eric's greatest strength – his incredible reflexes and feeling. While you're in the studio with Eric you might do the same song two or three different times and change key once or do it in two different tempos, and finally there's one magic moment where it's the right tempo and the right key and there's no question about it, but if you rehearsed that would not happen when you got in the studio, because it would be cut and dried and the spontaneity wouldn't be there.'

Understandably the years that had been hazed by heroin had not left a bulky backlog of ideas, but they hadn't been entirely barren, since 'little snippets of songs' survived. 'The past was like one big blank,' he admits. 'I'd got the impression that I'd done nothing in all that time, just sat and watched telly and never gone out or anything, but what I actually had done without realizing it was that I'd been putting on cassette after cassette and just playing, naturally keeping my hand in. So it wasn't all wasted at all.' And those snippets have served as occasional inspiration since.

That original shortlist of two contained Scott Boyer's 'Please Be With Me' and 'Give Me Strength', which he inaccurately credited to himself, though by default rather than dishonesty.

Beautiful as Boyer's song was, Clapton had another reason for wanting to record it: as a tribute to Duane Allman. 'He played some of the sweetest Dobro I've ever heard in my life on that, and I didn't really try that hard to emulate him, but I did my best. I always thought he was a finer Dobro player than he was electric slide player, because he had a lighter touch and more finesse.'

'Give Me Strength', according to Clapton, 'went back to when I used to live in a friend of mine's front room, and he had a great collection of records – just everything. And a lot of it was unlisted, just a reel-to-reel tape machine with compilation stuff, and it turned out that I picked up on that song, never found out who it was by, so I credited it to myself. It was a great song, because it was exactly what I was thinking about and feeling about at the time, and it came off straight away. It was obviously the key song to the album.' It's easy to see why Clapton felt so sympathetic to its lyric. Anyone coming off a habit as heavy as his would need to be strong, and he was praying to stay that way: 'Lord I've done so much wrong/But please give me strength to carry on.' More people than he knew said amen to that.

It was clear from the low-key acoustic feel of these two songs that in spite of several common factors (studio, producer, bass player, and Clapton himself) whatever was going down on tape was not another *Layla*, and Clapton sensed his public might not take too kindly to the prodigal returning without his characteristic chops. 'The groove we got into was getting so laid back, so quiet and delicate, that I just thought – no, they won't want to hear it.' So wisely he left the selection of tracks from the dozens they put down to Tom Dowd, who 'thought it would be better to have some of that and also some of the heavier stuff'.

The result was the balanced *461 Ocean Boulevard*, named after the address Clapton and the band stayed at during the recording. Only two tracks approached the energy level expected of an Eric Clapton album, the traditional 'Motherless Children' (rated by Clapton as the strongest track of the lot, yet never released as a single) and George Terry's 'Mainline Florida'. Elsewhere the mood hardly strayed outside an effortless groove, whether the material was his own ('Get Ready', cowritten with Yvonne Elliman, and 'Let It Grow'), blues (Elmore James' 'I Can't Hold Out' and Robert Johnson's 'Steady Rollin' Man'), fifties R&B (Johnny Otis' 'Willie And The Hand Jive') or reggae (Bob Marley and the Wailers' 'I Shot The Sheriff').

Like the recording of J. J. Cale's 'After Midnight' four years earlier, Clapton's cover of 'I Shot The Sheriff' was an event of some significance in his career, because reggae left an indelible mark on his music. And it gained greater significance still when RSO issued it as a single in July 1974 and the record went to No. 1 in the US charts, selling a million on the way. Although it was his first (and so far only) No. 1, Clapton's own attitude to 'I Shot The Sheriff' is ambivalent. If he'd had his way it wouldn't have been released as a single, wouldn't even have been included on the album, because he didn't think his version did justice to the original on the Wailers' *Burnin'* album. Nor does he take much credit for helping to put reggae – or J. J. Cale for that matter – on the musical map. 'I feel that's a bit indulgent to sit back and feel content about it,' he says. 'And what do you do when you meet the man? Pat him on the head and say, "Didn't I do you a good turn?" You've got to preserve a little bit of humility. I have to allow myself to think maybe he resents that in a way. It's a funny stance to take. I put myself in the firing line, because the artist who I'm covering can either resent me or feel grateful, and when I met Bob it wasn't very clear what he felt about it – if anything at all.'

Released in August, *461 Ocean Boulevard* was well received by the critics, whose general praise was only qualified by concern that fans of the familiar fireworks might feel let down. But if any did feel that way, it didn't show in the album's sales, which took it to the top of the US charts and to No. 3 in the UK.

By then, however, Clapton had already done a month of American dates, and in newspapers across the nation reviewers reacted rather differently to his concerts. At the opener in Yale 'when the band were bad, they were truly awful'; in Boston 'several songs moved with a deliberate, exaggerated slowness, giving cause to stretches of boredom'; the Washington performance was 'lethargic', Clapton's playing 'perfunctory'; the Los Angeles show was 'coolly professional, impressive at times, but only occasionally stirring ... tasteful, but not inspiring'; in New York he was 'stooped, scared, and looking stoned to someplace you don't want to think about'. And in December, when Clapton came on before a home crowd at the Hammersmith Odeon, it was apparent why critics and audiences alike felt frustrated.

Clapton's reaction to the old slogan bellowed from the stalls made it plain the man was through working miracles. 'I'm not bleedin' God', he assured the fan who'd been applauded for shouting that he was, 'I'm just a guitarist.' And a rhythm guitarist at that, he might have added, on the evidence of the ratio of strum to solo even when, several songs into the set, he put down his acoustic and strapped on his Strat.

Clearly what Clapton enjoyed best about being back on stage was playing in a band. Not in front of a band, but *in* a band. 'I refuse to be a bandleader,' he has said more than once. 'Just because they put my name – you know, Eric Clapton And His Band – well, I refuse to be bandleader. I'll take responsibility for certain things, but when it comes down to it, it's equal shares, and the responsibility, I'll take it because my name's on the top. But in terms of pulling everyone's weight, it's equal shares.' So he shared the singing with Yvonne Elliman and Marcy Levy (recruited during the American tour) and left a lot of the guitar solos to George Terry.

Ironically, Terry could copy the Clapton style accurately

enough to fool cheering sections of the crowd and people on the payroll too. 'It even comes down to, say, the lighting crew,' Clapton noted. 'They sometimes don't know, and I'll just be playing chords with George playing a solo, and they'll keep the spotlight on me, and I have to keep gesturing – over there, over *there*! I don't know what that means. I suppose we play pretty close style, but I can tell the difference.'

The impression that he was playing for his fellow musicians rather than the punters who'd paid to witness his return was heightened by his reluctance to address the audience and by a crop of false endings that were in-jokes on stage, but unappreciated elsewhere. And he has since admitted a measure of impatience in his attitude towards audiences: 'You find out pretty quickly if it's not going over and you're banging your head on a brick wall, so you play for the band.' Or: 'After a quarter of an hour if you're fed up with them shouting for a guitar solo, you give them a guitar solo, and that keeps them quiet. Then you get a request for a song and if you don't want to do that song you avoid it until you have to do it. You're actually pretty well chained to a live audience – you can't really fight them.' And: 'There's certain songs I do on stage, which I find very hard to do, I'm very nervous about, because they contain the softer side of my nature, and if I just hear one person shout out something in the middle of a ballad or something that is really giving me the chills to.play, I'll just turn off completely and get aggressive. I look at the exit lights, because they're always there – two green exit lights. One of these days I'm going to shoot the lot out with a shotgun. I just watch to see whether someone's going out or someone's coming in. It's like chipping away, it takes something out of me, a little bit out of me. It means I'm not holding that person in there, whatever I'm doing isn't good enough for him to sit still and listen right to the end, no matter how much he wants to take a leak.'

More than one music paper was unimpressed by Clapton's performance. 'When it came to the main event,' wrote *Record Mirror*'s reviewer, 'when the master picked up his instrument, his electric axe, there was nothing happening at all. The style was recognizable, the little sighing bends, the cutting force of blues passages, but his heart was not there. Even after much fine prompting from the second player, Clapton could still not get off. Add to that all the heavy spotlights, his ridiculously over-amplified guitar and all the breaks while he drank or smoked or adjusted his strap, and this event became a joke.'

But the most painful put-down came from Chris Welch, who had been chronicling Clapton's career in *Melody Maker* since the mid-sixties. Clapton committed the closing swipe to memory: 'I've seen better at Dingwalls.'

Nine

FURTHER ON UP THE ROAD

Clapton's progress in carving out a new career was involuntarily sporadic. If *There's One In Every Crowd*, released eight months after *461 Ocean Boulevard*, in April 1975, represented a second step along the route mapped out by its predecessor, he was frogmarched several steps back before the end of the year by his fans on one side and his record company on the other. In his eyes the universal acceptance of his comeback album had evidently meant as much as an audience on their feet for his new role of all-rounder, applauding for an encore. And more of the same is what his audience got, only more so.

There's One In Every Crowd was as low-key as its brown-framed monochrome sleeve, yet urbane and well-rounded, a more complete album than *461 Ocean Boulevard*. Whatever the style of the individual tracks, whether they were rock, reggae, blues or ballad, they all stuck to the same easy groove, and there were subtleties, like the almost inaudible 'Auld Lang Syne' mixed (on New Year's Eve) into the final fade on the second side, that echoed George Martin's arrangements for the Beatles. But as far as the diehards with Derek's licks still ringing in their ears were concerned, serenity and sophistication were unacceptable substitutes for solos that shook walls and rattled windows. (Typically, the record's one really dynamic guitar passage, on 'Better Make It Through Today', was counterbalanced by an organ break.) *There's One In Every Crowd* flopped. When the same thing had happened to *Layla*, Clapton had gone under. Now he faced its failure, although he couldn't hide the hurt entirely when he told an interviewer, 'I liked it as much [as *461 Ocean Boulevard*]. I didn't think it was an actual improvement, but then we were still getting to know one another. Initially it upset me quite a lot that *There's One In Every Crowd* didn't sell. A lot of emotional outlet had gone into that, a lot of expression. When you do something like that, like when a painter paints his masterpiece, he knows in the bottom of his heart that it's not going to sell because it's too emotional. But it's still upsetting. All you want to do is share it, that's all.'

Later he came to terms with the album's flaws, conceding, 'It's a good album, but it's nothing special really. The best parts of it are things that you'd have to listen for. It's the kind of record that if you didn't like it maybe after the third or fourth time, you wouldn't play it again, but if you did like it and you carried on listening to it, you'd hear things that were really fine, just little things in the background, little touches. But I wasn't disappointed, because I didn't think myself that we'd really done our best. Partly that was the changing of locations – starting it in one place, taking it to another, and then mixing it somewhere else. We started it in Jamaica, because it was the original idea of sunshine during the day and work during the night, and everyone just got lazy. We didn't even hear any reggae! It was like recording in Scunthorpe on a good day.'

Although Clapton was able eventually to shrug off the poor performance of *There's One In Every Crowd* with a line that was as throwaway as the album's title – 'It didn't do too well, but there you go' – RSO Records responded differently and quickly. Four months later, in August 1975, they had a live album out – against Clapton's wishes. 'I didn't want it out,' he recalls. 'There was a huge scandal going on at RSO, because I was trying to think of some way of actually getting it into the press that I denied any knowledge of it being me even. They're very much of the opinion that that is my forte – live albums – not in terms of artistry, but financial success. There was a long battle and I refused to let it go out until I heard I think it was 'Have You Ever Loved A Woman', and it was played to me by Tom Dowd in the studio – in Criteria – and he just said, "Listen to this," and the rest of it was built round that for me. He convinced me with that one track that it was worth doing a live album, and he had complete control over what went on there.

'I've been against live albums for a long time – there's very few that I've ever heard that've worked. What do you put on? If you've got some new numbers in the repertoire, even though they're good songs, they're probably shaky, because you haven't been doing them very long. So do you put them on because it's new material or do you choose an old faithful that's so easy to play you can do it with your eyes closed and therefore it comes out like a gem? It's a very difficult choice, and one that I don't particularly like, so I don't like doing live albums.

'With a studio album everything has to be new. You can't go in and do "Tell The Truth" or "Layla" – it's got to be new. With live albums it's always the same: we can't put this out *again*!'

But of course they could. Among the half dozen extended tracks on *E. C. Was Here* were four numbers familiar from studio recordings (Derek and the Domino's 'Have You Ever Loved A Woman', Blind Faith's 'Can't Find My Way Home' and 'Presence Of The Lord', and a throwback to Clapton's Bluesbreakers days, 'Ramblin' On My Mind'), two of which had already been recorded live – 'Have You Ever Loved A Woman' and 'Presence Of The Lord' on *Derek and the Dominos In Concert* and the latter on *Eric Clapton's Rainbow Concert* as well. And as further proof of the possibility, 'Ramblin' On My Mind' and 'Further On Up The Road' would reappear five years later on another live album, *Just One Night*. Still, there was always 'Drifting Blues'.

Aside from the Blind Faith songs, whose inclusion confirmed Clapton's continuing belief that *'Blind Faith* was a classic album', *E. C. Was Here* was the kind of album he could have cut in the sixties: blues played with bravura. It proved his chops were still in great shape, or had been on the dates that had been recorded, but precious little else. It was as if he hadn't made *461 Ocean Boulevard* or *There's One In Every Crowd*, as if the Band, J. J. Cale and Bob Marley were undiscovered influences, as if he had never been away, nor come back. It was a sop to the loudmouths who shouted at the stage between songs for a solo they knew by heart anyway. It was RSO executives pushing the panic button. It was Eric Clapton being beaten by the business *again*. It was a cop-out.

Curiously, listening to the album later, Clapton was mostly concerned about his vocal performance. 'The voice still isn't improving,' he complained, 'But only time will tell. I don't like sounding like a young man. I like high-sounding voices coming from other people, but I don't like the sound of mine myself. I like a mid-range to come out of me. If you're singing a blues like 'Have You Ever Loved A Woman', the ultimate kind of sound to reach is something like Freddie King or B. B. King, where they don't actually sing a high note, they scream it. It's like a rasp and although it's high it sounds mid-range. It's the same note, but they put a lot of growl into it. I suppose you could call it a split octave, that would be a technical way of putting it, but it's just that they're using all their lungs and I wasn't there.'

When *E. C. Was Here* appeared, Clapton was already on the road again in America. The acoustic opening had been abandoned; instead he stopped the shouting by doing 'Layla' at the off. And there was a new song in the set – an August released, reggaed-up cover of Bob Dylan's 'Knockin' On Heaven's Door', which was strikingly similar to a version that had come out less than a fortnight before by Jamaican Arthur Louis, on which

Clapton himself could be heard. Clapton's choice of Louis' 'Someone Like You' for his own B-side suggested a trade, though in fact neither version was a hit.

The previous summer Clapton's first tour in almost four years had been a riotous caravan in the established manner of rock and roll's privileged pranksters, but this time life off stage was less of a lark, while the patient policing of Clapton showed not everyone was convinced his cure was permanent. 'It's a drag,' he told *NME*'s Nick Logan, 'because I am thirty years of age, and I believe I have a right to make my own decisions. If I take it onto myself to go out and score some hard drugs then that is my right. But that is beside the point: the fact is it just separates me from the band. They feel they are just like sidemen, that I'm the superstar with the suite. It'll probably change sooner or later. But it's not going to change yet, because they still don't trust me. I don't know, there's not much I can do about it. It's very difficult. I sneak off whenever I can, but there's always somebody watching me.'

By the end of that American tour Clapton's band had been together as long as Cream, yet few fans could rattle off a roll-call of its members, a lapse that irritated the leader. 'On behalf of the band I feel very annoyed,' he explained, 'because there's no reason they shouldn't be superstars too, because they're all good. But every time someone asks me what I'm doing and I tell them I'm just generally working or keeping a low profile or going on tour, they say, "Oh, are you with the same band?" And I say, "Yeah, of course," and they say, "Well, who's in it now?" And I have to reel off the names. I don't think after all this time it should be necessary.'

As it was, the band went on to complete two more albums before the first major upheaval occurred with the departure of Yvonne Elliman the following summer to pursue a solo career on the strength of two US top twenty hits with 'Love Me' and 'Hello Stranger', a decision soon vindicated by a million-selling American No. 1 in May 1978 with 'If I Can't Have You' from the *Saturday Night Fever* soundtrack.

The one significant change in Clapton's recording habits was brought about by external circumstances, when Atlantic Records reacted to RSO's ending of their long-standing association by preventing producers under contract to Atlantic from working with RSO acts, a ban which stopped Tom Dowd producing Clapton (and separated Arif Mardin and the Bee Gees).

Unwillingly deprived of his first choice producer, Clapton opted for a more informal approach than the patriarchal Dowd would have encouraged, recording at Shangri-la, a former whorehouse beside Pacific Coast Highway in Malibu, California, which had been converted into a studio by the Band. Its atmosphere appealed to Clapton immediately.

'It was great,' he recalls, 'because it was all wood and the room you record in was originally a master bedroom or a playroom – because it was a bordello it probably had about twenty waterbeds in – and it had a couple of sliding doors that you could just leave open to the outside with the sea not more than a hundred feet away, lapping on the beach, and you would record like that and that would go on the machine. It was something you couldn't do anywhere else – that was it. It was a very special place.'

The sessions themselves were often open house, a situation which might have upset his regular rhythm section, though, according to Clapton, 'They never said anything – but Tulsa musicians in LA behave very strangely. They tend to get very lazy or want to knock around. The Band actually owning the studio, they were there most of the time, and Rick Danko, who's a real hustler, would be there trying to push songs or something, so I'd just have to show up there and they'd be ready to play – and my own band would still be by the pool, so it just happened. They never said anything, but I think it's all right and I think it worked out okay. I just think it was misinterpreted by the people that reviewed it.

'One of the reviews, I think it was either *Rolling Stone* or *Creem*, said I was "cronying" – hanging out and getting everyone to play on the record – and actually it was true, but it was a very, very strong time for the studio, because it had been empty and it hadn't been used and suddenly all these people showed up from nowhere, like Billy Preston and Van Morrison, and it was very hard to get any work done, because people kept walking in and picking up instruments and just playing, so it's got that on it and if that's wrong, well, fuck it! But I thought it was very good, it was a very healthy time.

'And I'll tell you another thing that blew me away. It was the first time the band had played together for about a year, and it took us coming in there to get them all in the studio with one another, because there was a lot of bitching. So it was very valuable from that point of view too. Richard Manuel and I would always end up being the last people at the session, having pissed everybody else off, out of our brains playing a song that Little Walter cut called, "Last Night I Lost The Best Friend I Ever Had" – I've got hundreds of versions of that on tape.

'If you're working with serious professional musicians, who can get drunk and still play and not fall over.... And if you can play it all night until eight in the morning and still know the chords of the song, you're a professional musician.

'Right in the middle of the sessions I had a magnificent birthday party [30 March], and we decided to record everything and everybody that came into the studio. I've got copies of it on reel-to-reel. It's got Billy Preston singing a couple of Ray Charles songs with the Band backing him and Jesse Ed Davis, me, Robbie [Robertson] and Woody [Ron Wood] on guitars – superb stuff. Dylan showed up about eight in the morning and it just went on from there – new songs he was making up, arguments about this and that, like "Who wrote that one?", and lots of gossip about other musicians. We dissected the Beatles one by one. He's a very funny character. All he needs is a word to spark him off and he'll get really sort of intense and won't give a shit what he's saying, and you just sit there amazed that this guy's being so outrageous. And then he'll just flip into a song and it's all forgotten and you carry on. It's really hot bootleg material.'

Despite Clapton's claim that it was very hard to get any work done at Shangri-la, the sessions were productive – 'something like twenty-five tracks in three weeks out of nowhere, out of the blue, it was just like falling rain. And the outtakes – whoever's got them is sitting on a mint, because they're beautiful. Some of the best stuff didn't get on the album.'

The basic tracks were engineered by the Band's sound man, but once they were down Clapton brought in Rob Fraboni to supervise the overdubs and, more importantly, the mixing, an operation he himself avoids at all costs. 'I can't stand it at all,' he admits. 'You get a bad taste in your mouth from hearing the same thing, especially if you're conscious of very small mistakes. By the time you've heard it over and over again, it makes you want to scrap the song for that one thing, so I don't ever turn up at those deals.'

Anyone acquainted with the material only as it appeared on record would be none the wiser, but according to Clapton there was an audible change between the tracks as they went down and as they were mastered. 'It was a shame Rob came in so late,' he said with hindsight. 'Because he wasn't there when we recorded it, it was a bit disjointed. We'd recorded lots and lots of tracks with lots of guide vocals and I left it to him to pick out what he thought was best. It was really rough, but I enjoyed that kind of feeling about it. I've got the original mixes of side one somewhere, and they're unbelievably different. They're great. And it's a shame, because Rob came in in a different studio, and if he'd been able to mix it in Shangri-la it would've kept that original feel. But we had to take it to Village Recorders and mix it there in a totally different atmosphere, and it lost a little. It gained a little, but it wasn't the same as the original concept.'

The credits, when *No Reason To Cry* was released in August 1976, read, 'This album was produced by Rob Fraboni in association with Eric Clapton and Carl Dean Radle,' and the list of musicians included, besides Clapton's own band, Rick Danko, Levon Helm, Garth Hudson, Richard Manuel and Robbie Robertson of the Band, Jesse Ed Davis, Bob Dylan, Georgie Fame, Albhy Galuten, George Harrison, Chris Jagger, Billy Preston, percussionist Sergio Pastora Rodriguez (who stayed with Clapton for his next tour), Wah Wah Watson, and Ronnie Wood. And yet this undisciplined band of irregulars created a remarkably coherent album.

Whether he was trading verses with Rick Danko on their 'All Our Past Times', sharing a scratchy harmony with Bob Dylan on the latter's 'Sing Language', being supported by Yvonne Elliman and Marcy Levy on 'Hello Old Friend', 'Carnival' and 'Hungry' (three songs which, along with the delicate closing ballad, 'Black Summer Rain', were instantly recognizable as post-comeback Clapton), dipping back into the blues bag for the relaxed 'County Jail Blues' or a fiery performance of Otis Rush's 'Double Trouble' that brought back memories from ten years before, whether he was backed by the Tulsa team or the Band, and whether it was he, or Ron Wood, Robbie Robertson or George Terry on guitar, Clapton was permanently present, nudging the music in the direction he wanted it to go. As when he'd recorded his first solo album in 1970 with Delaney and Bonnie's band, however diffident he acted outwardly, apparently content to let things happen, he was making the most of the musicians who showed up at Shangri-la.

The one song Clapton didn't sing, Marcy Levy's vocal showcase, 'Innocent Times', which he cowrote with her, gave the album its title, though only after he'd turned her lyric around. '"With no freedom to laugh, there's more reason to cry" was her line on the record,' he pointed out, 'but I decided it should be "*no* reason to cry".'

That he allowed Levy a solo spot on his album, as he did Yvonne Elliman on stage, was proof of the pleasure Clapton got from playing with both women, because their recruitment had been no more than grudgingly accepted by some sections of his audience, more noticeably so in Britain than America, where the gospel-based harmonies and call-and-response interplay were not only rooted in religious tradition, but had been incorporated into popular music too by R&B singers like Ray Charles (with his Raelets) as long ago as the fifties and into an influential area of white rock at the end of the sixties by Delaney and Bonnie, whose impact on a circle of singers that stretched from Joe Cocker to Kris Kristofferson had been no less profound than on Clapton himself.

But Clapton demanded more of his singers than their vocal abilities. Both could strum an acoustic, rattle maracas or bang a tambourine, and Levy blew mouth harp, so they earned their equal status in the band. 'In every sense they're real people – musicians too, that's the thing,' he explained after Elliman's departure. 'They were very strong, very strong indeed. It was a great temptation for me to walk off the stage and let them have half an hour each, because they could've done it, being multi-instrumentalists and what have you.' But when Elliman left, she was not replaced; nor, when Levy followed her in 1978, was she. A ritual washing of hands, and that was it; not even a half glance back. As he put it in the song he wrote with Rick Danko: 'All our past times should be forgotten, all our past times should be erased.'

In fact, in his entire career it's hard to count more than one occasion when Clapton has made a break and then recanted: the time he quit John Mayall and took off for Greece with the Glands, but was back in the Bluesbreakers three months later. Every other move has been irrevocable, and usually unforeseen. Like when he left the Yardbirds in the lurch in 1965; or the Bluesbreakers for the second, decisive time in 1966 and Mayall heard about it the way everyone else did – from *Melody Maker*; and though Cream's end was a communal decision, Blind Faith's was Clapton's doing, likewise Derek's dropping of the Dominos. Even sticking with a musician between one band and the next, as with Ginger Baker, was exceptional, while his relationship with Carl Radle remains his longest association with any musician. Clapton first came across him in Delaney and Bonnie's backing band and used him on his first solo album and again in Derek and the Dominos, and it was Radle he cabled and Radle who came running when he reemerged in 1974. 'Radle saw Elliman and Levy come and go, survived George Terry's departure and Albert Lee's arrival, and must have been about ready for a long-service medal, when Clapton suddenly dropped the Tulsa trio. Radle died soon after of an overdose.

Yvonne Elliman's final stint with the band was in the studio, recording Clapton's best-selling album since he was in Cream, *Slowhand*. Its success was unexpected, not least to Clapton himself. 'I mean, what was there to it?', comes the rhetorical question. 'Laid-back is not the word for it, it was almost limp. *Layla* wasn't a success, it died a death, but, as far as I was

concerned, I'd've put that album up against anybody's that was
out at the time. With *Slowhand* it was a completely different
story. It was lightweight, really lightweight, and the reason for
that, I think, is partly due to the fact that some of the stuff that
we wanted to put on the record I wrote, say, six months before.
We were on the road and we wrote some songs and got to the
studio, and we couldn't get to the studio early enough – we
wanted a couple of weeks off or something like that – and by the
time we got in there, everyone knew the song so well, we were so
sort of limp about it that it was lazy.'

The studio was Olympic in southwest London, favoured by
Glyn Johns, an English producer whose credits include the
Rolling Stones, the Who, the Faces, the Eagles, brought by him
to the Barnes studio early in their career, and the Pete
Townshend/Ronnie Lane collaboration, *Rough Mix*, to which
Clapton had recently contributed. However, Johns' approach to
record production didn't always coincide with Clapton's and the
atmosphere at sessions could be uncomfortable. The choice of
songs – Clapton's own as well as those from outside sources – was
one area where artist and producer didn't see eye to eye, as
instanced by the Troy Seals/Eddie Setser composition, 'Black
Rose', which was rejected by Johns even though Clapton considered it a beautiful song, an opinion he still held three years
later when, reunited with Tom Dowd, he recorded it for *Another
Ticket*. Nevertheless, the nine tracks that eventually emerged as
Slowhand were a reasonable representation of the state of Eric
Clapton's art in 1977.

It opened with a future crowd-pleaser, J. J. Cale's 'Cocaine', the
inclusion of a song by an acknowledged influence less surprising
than the reason Clapton covered it: 'I recorded it because he
nicked the "Sunshine Of Your Love" riff. It was a straight lift and
I told him. I said, "Look, man, you don't mind me doing this, but
you *did* nick that riff." And it was pretty fucking obvious.'

Cale happened to be playing in London while *Slowhand* was
being recorded, so the band took a break from their sessions to
go and see him perform at the New Victoria. 'He was so good,'
Clapton recalls, 'it was just like the record except he didn't play
it the same. It was the same intensity. We stood in the wings and
watched him and *whispered* to each other. It was really good. His
guitar is unbelievable – it's got no back on it. It's an old acoustic
with about eight pick-ups and they all work, and he gets this
amazing combination of sounds out of it. He can get a wah-wah
out of it without using a pedal, for instance. He's a real genius
with electronics. If he holds the guitar against himself he gets a
different sound, and if he takes it away from his body he gets a

different sound, because there's no back to it.

'We brought him down to the studio to listen to "Cocaine", to see what he thought of our version of it, and he liked it – because I wasn't exactly sure what he was singing and I wanted to get the words straight with him as well. And he got us to go and play with him at the New Vic. So me and Carl, I think it was, went on and joined in and played "Cocaine".'

Although 'Cocaine' was the only Cale song on *Slowhand*, the influence of 'the subtlest character around' was apparent elsewhere on the album, especially on 'Lay Down Sally', a song written by Clapton and Marcy Levy whose feel owed everything to the relaxed, relentless Tulsa rhythms Delaney Bramlett had originally turned him on to, and, according to Clapton, 'It's as close as I can get, being English, but the band being a Tulsa band, they play like that naturally. You couldn't get them to do an English rock sound – no way. Their idea of a driving beat isn't being loud or anything, it's subtle.' Perhaps that gap between musical sensibilities on either side of the Atlantic explains why 'Lay Down Sally' barely dented the UK top forty when it was released as a single, but went to No. 3 in the US, where it sold a million.

Another influence had emerged alongside Cale in the shape of Texan country singer Don Williams, who had had a British hit in 1976, following his performance at the Wembley Festival, with 'I Was Born A Gypsy Woman', a five-year-old record which in retrospect would obviously have appealed to the 'new' Clapton. When Williams visited Britain as a result of that hit, Clapton turned up at the opening show in Croydon, invited him and his band back to his house afterwards, and sat in the next night at Hammersmith. (Later, when Clapton played Nashville's Municipal Auditorium in 1978, he asked Williams to open the show.) On *Slowhand* he affirmed his admiration by recording Williams' 'We're All The Way'.

Both the song and the performance were emphatically low-key, as was the acoustic strumalong 'May You Never', written by John Martyn, another recently absorbed influence, although the Scottish guitarist had been recording since the late sixties, and even the obligatory blues, 'Mean Old Frisco', was steady rather than inspired. Add to them Clapton's intriguingly vengeful, but even-paced 'Next Time You See Her' and 'Peaches And Diesel', an easy instrumental cowritten by Clapton and Albhy Galuten (a keyboard player who'd been on *461 Ocean Boulevard*), and all that was left to raise the listener's pulse was 'The Core', written and sung with Marcy Levy, on which Clapton's voice recalled Jack Bruce and his playing, towards the end, his old explosive self.

Yet the album's most memorable moments were its most
intimate, as Clapton sang a love song to his girlfriend Patti,
which was so empty of artifice and full of real feeling that he'd
been uncertain how it would be accepted in the studio. 'Christ
almighty, with a band like mine which is really a hard rock band
when it comes down to it, who like nothing more than to hit a
groove and stay there, to present them with a song like that on
your second day in the studio, and they've never heard it before,
you can't imagine what they must be thinking,' he admitted.
'And then you do it and they all say it's marvellous – they're all
real softies at heart.'

In 'Wonderful Tonight' Clapton had created a perfect love
song, if perfection is articulating a universally recognizable
emotion in a way no one else has and stating it in a sympathetic
musical setting, although with characteristic self-deprecation he
once dismissed its theme thus: 'It was just about taking the old
woman out and getting too sloshed to drive home.' Seven years
before, falling in love with Patti had given rise to the turbulent
passion of 'Layla', but now he and she were long-time lovers, and
he was hit by a sudden surge of feeling. 'Every now and then you
fall in love again, albeit with the same woman,' he explained,
'just one night for some reason – something she's said or the way
she's approached the situation, and bang! you're in love again,
and it's such a strong feeling you can't do anything else but write
it down. Situations of that extremity don't happen every day – if
they did then I'd be the most prolific writer in the world. They
only happen every two or three months, but there you go. That's
why a song is moving, because you don't think what the diction
is like or how clever the words should be or how well they should
rhyme, it's just like you're saying something to somebody, as if
you're in conversation with them. I like listening to story type
songs, parable type things with morals, but the songs that
always hit me most are the ones where I actually recognize what
the guy is talking about and it's as if he's talking to me or
someone that I know or something like that. It's like a conversation coming out of the record player.' It was Clapton's favourite song on the album, and as a single gave him another US top
twenty hit when it reached No. 16 in July 1978.

Because *Slowhand* was such a massive commercial success,
Clapton returned to Olympic in August, once again with Glyn
Johns as producer, but although the circumstances were the
same, he didn't plan a repeat performance. 'I used to think the
way to record an album was to top what you'd done before,' he
said later, 'but it doesn't work. It never works, because what
you've done before is in the past, and that's that. If you try and

emulate what you've done before, then you're in a rut, and you might as well wave goodbye to the future altogether. So I didn't try.'

The album appeared in November, its title, *Backless*, an allusion to Bob Dylan, whom Clapton had supported at an open-air concert at Blackbushe four months before. According to Clapton, 'It became very apparent that he knew exactly what was going on everywhere around him all the time. I mean, if you were backstage, he expected you to be putting as much into it as he was. You couldn't just stand there and be one of the roadies, you had to actually focus all your attention on him, and if you didn't, he knew it, and he'd turn round and he'd look at you and you'd get daggers.'

Clapton's regard for Dylan is considerable: more, as that anecdote suggests, then one musician's respect for another. Even being told you're the best guitarist in the world doesn't mean not being in awe of Bob Dylan, it seems, especially when it's Dylan who's doing the telling. 'He can say something like, "I think you're the best guitarist in the world," and you think, Does he really? And you'll see a look on his face which means that he's putting you on or he wants you to think he's putting you on, so the only thing to do is ignore it. The only way I've ever been able to communicate with him is on a very jovial level. I couldn't imagine talking to him seriously about anything – he's got too much humour.'

Their relationship dates from an abortive recording session at Chappell's Bond Street Studio in London when Clapton was with John Mayall and Dylan and his producer Tom Wilson were both drunk. Between takes of 'If You Gotta Go, Go Now', the Bluesbreakers' drummer Hughie Flint could be heard remarking, 'You've not worked much with bands.' More recently they played together at Bob Dylan's Wembley Stadium concert in July 1984, when Clapton walked out on stage, plugged in, and then stood there amazed as Dylan turned his back on 75,000 fans while he taught him the chords to 'Señor'.

Dylan contributed two songs to *Backless*, 'Walk Out In The Rain' and 'If I Don't Be There By Morning', both cowritten with Helena Springs, though the only obvious evidence of Dylan's involvement was his name in the credits. Elsewhere there was the earthy 'I'll Make Love To You Anytime' by J. J. Cale, seemingly by now as permanent a presence on Clapton's albums as Robert Johnson had been in the sixties, an era that was echoed in a blues that could have come from the back room of a London pub during the R&B boom, the traditional 'Early In The Morning', while Don Williams' guitarist Danny Flowers provided the rousing 'Tulsa Time'. Williams' own influence could be heard in the understated approach to 'Promises', which gave Clapton another US top ten hit in January 1979. Clapton's compositions ranged from the good-time cautionary tale 'Watch Out For Lucy', through Marcy Levy's solo vocal spot, 'Roll It', which was as much a showcase for slide guitar and surely evolved in the studio, to the customary love songs.

If 'Tell Me That You Love Me' was prompted by nothing more particular than a reluctance to allow that kind of emotional complacency which occurs periodically in a long-term relationship to set in, 'Golden Ring', the album's most beautiful song, was inspired by specific circumstances. Like 'Wonderful Tonight' it was an open page in the emotional diary of Eric Clapton, the entry a result of Patti's reaction to her ex-husband George Harrison's remarriage – 'It all went well and suddenly then you heard that he was married again' – and concluding in a question: 'If I gave to you a golden ring, would I make you happy?' That question, slipped into a song, was made concrete before too long, and Eric and Patti married in April 1979 during a tour of the Southern States. On their return they sent out silver-edged invitations, although the wording was less than formal: 'Me and the Mrs got married the other day, but that was in America, so we've decided to have a bash in my garden on Saturday May 19th for all our mates here at home.' Since their mates included some illustrious musicians the small stage in the flower-filled marquee supported an all-star line-up the like of which hadn't been seen since the Band's farewell concert in San Francisco in 1976 and before that the Bangla Desh show in 1971. The cause on this occasion was having a good time and the repertoire a collection of oldies they'd all learned more years before than they probably cared to remember. But when had three Beatles last shared a stage? Or Clapton, Bruce and Baker?

Clapton himself felt 'Golden Ring' was the strongest song on the album, and not simply because of its theme. 'I was fed up with the general sort of apathy of everyone involved,' he recalls, 'and I just thought, Well, I'll take a song in there and whether they like it or not, I'll do it, and they'll learn it and they'll record it, and we'll put it on the record, and that's that! And that kind of conviction carried the thing through. I spoke to Don Williams just before Christmas – he called up to say "Happy Christmas and God bless the folks" – and I said that I liked his album and "Tulsa Time" and everything, and he said that "Golden Ring" was his favourite track too. Because it was the only one that came through with any kind of feeling – with strength. And if you listen to it, there's virtually nothing on it.' What there was on it

were vocal harmonies from Benny Gallagher and Graham Lyle
(as well as an uncredited accordion that could have been either):
proof of his fondness for a duo who had turned down his offer of a
tour support spot a couple of years before, but also perhaps a
shred of evidence that he was tiring of the same sounds behind
him.

Interviewed in December 1978 on a British tour that followed
the release of *Backless*, he was asked by *Melody Maker*'s Chris
Welch why he had worked with American musicians throughout
the seventies. 'Well, they're the best,' Clapton replied. 'I think
they play better than most British musicians. The only two I've
met who can come anywhere near Jamie and Carl are Dave
Markee and Henry Spinetti. I think they're fine. But they're
session musicians, studio men. The Americans understand more
about what has influenced me.' The plug for Markee and Spinetti
took up two dozen words among several thousand and didn't
sound like the rustle of a new leaf about to flip over, but by the
time Clapton was on stage in Japan a year later they'd replaced
Radle and Oldaker, and Dick Sims had gone besides.

The line-up for the tour at the end of 1978 was the first four-
piece Clapton had been in since Derek and the Dominos, George
Terry and Marcy Levy having departed in August after the
Backless sessions, and he found handling all the guitar work
himself unsatisfactory. 'The four-piece line-up worked out on
some songs,' he said after the tour's end, 'but it didn't work out
on the others. There were others where there were just holes and
I felt I was doing too much. And if I go to see a guitar player, I
don't like to see him doing everything, playing the chords and
then playing the lead, I like to see it balanced out.'

A highlight of the tour for Clapton was having Muddy Waters
as opening act. Although in his sixties, the Mississippi bluesman
had abandoned none of the braggadocio or the machismo of the
Mannish Boy who mobilized a legion of British musicians in the
early sixties. His energy was undiminished on stage and his
performances could be so cathartic that Clapton preferred not to
see them. 'I can't,' he admitted. 'I did a couple of times, I stood in
the wings and watched him, and by the time it was my turn to go
on stage I was so completely exhausted that I just couldn't
follow him. So we ended up getting to the gig just in time for us to
go on stage, so I wouldn't see any of his set. It must be
exhilarating for the audience, so they were probably exhausted
by the time we walked on, because he *really* puts it out.'

Less memorable was the footage shot on the Continental tour
that preceded the UK dates. Clapton had reason to be wary of
film crews since, ten years before, Cream had allowed cameras at

their Royal Albert Hall farewell show, and he, and Jack Bruce and Ginger Baker had each been interviewed on camera. By the time the film was screened as *Cream's Last Concert* on BBC2's *Omnibus* in January 1969 director Tony Palmer had nobbled the project with a voice-over by Patrick Allen that was so absurdly pretentious it sounded like a send-up. This time the problem was a different one. Less self-conscious, it was actually uninteresting. The concert footage was ordinary, while the offstage scenes only emphasized what a tedious business touring is, even on a special train, and there was certainly nothing new to be learned from the film about its central subject. Assembled for a private showing, it appealed to its participants the way home movies do, but it was shelved before it was seen by a wider audience.

Clapton's attitude to touring is ambivalent. As he's contemplated a tour schedule, he's said, 'I like it now, but I won't like it for the first week because I'll have the itinerary with me and I'll be going "Oh, no!" And then the last week'll come and I'll be going "Oh, no!" because it's coming to an end.' But as he'll happily admit to being lazy – 'I think all musicians are lazy, I think that's one of the best parts about us' – he needs a reason to get out on the road. 'I could survive, I imagine, on my royalties,' he speculates, 'but the minute I stop thinking how's the money coming in, it's just too easy then. I've got to force myself into a position where I think if I don't go out and play, I'll go broke. Because playing isn't everything. You've got your home life, you build up a little kind of empire – your house and a woman and people that depend on you. You can't just lie back, you've got to pretend that you're actually on the verge of bankruptcy, so that you can go out and graft. Otherwise you just sit back and get fat and do fuck all.

'The real dilemma is that you have to face up to management trying to convince you all the time that you never have to do another thing in your life if you don't want to. That's what I get from Robert (Stigwood) every time I see him: "If you don't want to do it, you can pack it in now, you don't have to do another thing, you're secure for the rest of your life." And that's the *last* thing I want to hear – it's like I'm out to pasture. I don't ever want to be broke again – nobody wants that – but I've got to keep myself in preparation for it mentally and spiritually somehow, even if it means creating a fantasy. And in actual fact I do get more money going out on the road than I do from records, and that's always an incentive.'

So it was that he was back on tour before too long: ten days in Ireland in mid-March followed by forty-six American dates between then and the end of June – three and a half months on

the road with a three-week break in May. The shortcomings of
the four-piece line-up had been alleviated by the arrival of Albert
Lee, an exceptionally accomplished guitarist who had played
the same club circuit in the mid-sixties with Chris Farlowe's
Thunderbirds as Clapton had with the Yardbirds and John
Mayall's Bluesbreakers, but had traded his blues licks for
country picking, eventually taking over from the legendary
American James Burton in Emmylou Harris' Hot Band in 1976.
When Clapton's personal manager Roger Forrester suggested
Lee, according to Clapton, 'it was just like bang! – light bulb –
and I thought, Why didn't I think of that?'

The first album with Lee in the line-up was *Just One Night*,
recorded live at the Budokan Theatre in Tokyo in December
1979, and by then the Tulsa trio of Radle, Oldaker and Sims had
been replaced by Dave Markee, Henry Spinetti and keyboard
player Chris Stainton. Discounting the Rainbow concert, this
was the first time Clapton had worked with British musicians
since Blind Faith, and he had frequently repeated his opinion
that Americans played his kind of music better. Occasionally,
though, he'd touched on the problem of leading a band that lived
on the other side of the Atlantic; as he put it, 'We don't get to
groove enough.' And Clapton loves to groove, to play for the
pleasure of making music with other musicians, not for an
audience or the box-office take, but for those moments when
everyone locks together.

Just One Night showed a subtle but perceptible shift in the
sound that surrounded Clapton's guitar and voice. Spinetti's
drumming was more solidly insistent than Oldaker's, Markee's
bass busier than Radle's, Stainton's keyboards showier than
Sim's steady textures, but above all Albert Lee was a more
effective foil than Terry had been. Often Terry's role had been to
cover for Clapton, to pass off solos in his style when the front
man wasn't up to it, and he could do it well enough to fool
unobservant audiences, but Lee had spent too long perfecting a
style of his own, one of those rare few in rock that are always
recognizable, to copy Clapton. His contribution was closer to
Duane Allman's on *Layla*, to carry on a kind of conversation
between Clapton's guitar and his own, and by his own eloquence
and invention inspire the other's repartee. The fact that his vocal
harmonies were good enough to have got him a gig with Don
Everly singing Phil's parts when the brothers weren't on terms
was a bonus, and his reward on *Just One Night* was a solo spot on
Mark Knopfler's 'Setting Me Up'.

Whereas *E. C. Was Here* had contained no trace of Clapton's
two previous studio albums, more than half the material on *Just*

One Night came from *Backless, Slowhand* and *No Reason To Cry*, showing that the split between his stage and studio personae was less pronounced now. Only two years before he'd said, 'Unless you go and see a concert, buying a record isn't really going to be any reference to what I'm doing at all. The studio is of secondary importance. I used to think that that was it, that was your record – a record of all your achievements that would never die – but I don't think so any more. I think that's just something you have to do for posterity – say, "Okay, this is this year's attitude" – but it's got nothing to do with how you treat a different set of individuals. You're not playing to anyone in the studio, you're playing to an imaginary audience. So you have to make up your mind what they're like, and it's usually yourself you end up facing. So you play for yourself and put what you want to hear on the record and that's that, but when you're actually stuck in a live environment then you just try every angle.

'We always cassette shows and if I don't listen to them while we're doing the tour I'll inevitably check it out when I get home. And some things are just embarrassingly long when you listen to them sitting down at home. It's too long or too loud and you don't get any excitement of the presence of the place, but there's no doubt in my mind that at the time you were doing it, it was the right thing to do. I don't think anyone in the audience would have had any complaint about the length of it – they probably would've liked it to have been longer. That is unalterable, it's just bending with the people and making it work, so everyone leaves with a certain amount of satisfaction.'

Besides the versions of his recent studio recordings, there were two songs from his very first solo album – 'After Midnight' and 'Blues Power' – and two from John Mayall's Bluesbreakers' repertoire, 'Ramblin' On My Mind' (which slipped into 'Have You Ever Loved A Woman' and out again) and 'Further On Up The Road', a favourite he had also performed at the Band's farewell concert, billed and filmed as *The Last Waltz*. The one unfamiliar number was Big Maceo Merriweather's Chicago blues standard from the forties, 'Worried Life Blues'. Only his antipathy towards live albums could have prevented Clapton from feeling satisfied with *Just One Night*, because he was playing and singing as well as he ever had.

In 1980 he found himself free to work with Tom Dowd again and took his band, now enlarged by the addition of former Procol Harum keyboard player and vocalist Gary Brooker, to Compass Point Studios in the Bahamas to record *Another Ticket*. Apart from the absence of any female voice, the sound of the album was

what separated it most obviously from the studio recordings
done without Dowd, because the material was the expected mix
of blues, country, rock and ballads. Overall it was cleaner, more
precise, and the songs were arranged more elaborately and the
production was more polished than anything since *There's One
In Every Crowd*. Clapton played with taste and authority, and
his singing was more self-consciously expressive than his usual
relaxed, even throwaway vocal delivery.

It was hard to find fault with an album that was so carefully
executed and accomplished, what it lacked being what Clapton
himself had lost: the fire of youth. But then again, Muddy
Waters, whose 'Blow Wind Blow' was included in homage, kept
that flame aglow until the end of his life. Clapton's guitar only
sparked occasionally, and when it didn't it was evidently a
matter of choice. As the world-weary title track suggested,
Another Ticket was the work of a man in his mid-thirties,
resigned to the onset of middle age.

And there were reminders of a younger Clapton in *Steppin'
Out*, a compilation of mid-sixties Decca material released in
1981, and in *Timepieces*, a 1982 RSO album subtitled *The Best Of
Eric Clapton*, which went back as far as his 1970 recordings of
'After Midnight' and 'Layla', the concurrent reissue of the latter
as a single underlining its enduring class when it reached No. 4
that April.

Of the band that made *Another Ticket* only Albert Lee survived to play on *Money And Cigarettes* in 1983, contributing
keyboards as well as guitar to the sessions at Compass Point in a
line-up of experienced American session men: Ry Cooder, whose
reputation as a slide guitarist stemmed as much from his solo
albums as from his work for the Rolling Stones, Randy Newman
and the rest; Memphis bass man Donald 'Duck' Dunn, former
member of Booker T. and the MGs and a mainstay of the Stax
sound of the sixties; and drummer Roger Hawkins from the
South's other major recording centre, Muscle Shoals, who with
the rest of the Fame studio rhythm section had been coopted by
Traffic in the seventies.

If the opening track, Sleepy John Estes' 'Everybody Oughta
Make A Change', sounded like an apologia for the new company
Clapton was keeping, his own 'Ain't Going Down' contained a
more telling argument: 'If I had my way, I would probably just sit
and stare/Watch the TV or read a book I'd have no reason to be
aware/But I ain't got time, I just could not live that way/I've got
to step outside myself, I've still got something left to say.' The
album certainly proved he had a lot left to play, for the guitar
work was genuinely potent, more consistently so than in a long

time. It was tempting to conclude that at this stage in his career he needed a prod from musicians of the calibre of Cooder, Lee, Dunn and Hawkins to get up enough to cut it.

Some Eric Clapton albums with as many tracks as the ten on *Money And Cigarettes* had left the impression of being light on material, but the variety and construction of the current crop of songs filled both sides with plenty of music, while the mood, buoyed by the novelty R&B of Johnny Otis's 'Crazy Country Hop', the salacious double entendre of 'Crosscut Saw' and the happy affirmation of 'I've Got A Rock And Roll Heart' and 'Man In Love', was unmistakably up. And as a personal insight into Clapton's own state of mind, *Money And Cigarettes* not only contained the latest chapter in the touchingly eternal love story of El and Nell in 'Pretty Girl', but also confirmation in 'The Shape You're In' that although his wife might still enjoy a drink, he was now teetotal, a state he has stuck to determinedly.

The Eric Clapton who strode onto the stage of the Royal Albert Hall on 20th September 1983, five weeks short of fifteen years since he'd said goodbye there to Cream, was an impressively healthy looking man, in better shape no doubt than Bruce or Baker would have looked if they'd been reunited with him that night. As it was, the musicians performing there took the mind back beyond Cream, because amongst the assembled stars were Clapton's successors in the Yardbirds, Jeff Beck and Jimmy Page. The reason they were there, along with Rolling Stones Bill Wyman and Charlie Watts, the Who's Kenney Jones, Stevie Winwood and others, was to raise money for Action Research into Multiple Sclerosis, the crippling disease that had ravaged their friend and fellow musician Ronnie Lane. (A repeat performance took place the next night in aid of the Prince of Wales Trust.) Clapton opened the show, which included separate sets by Winwood, Beck and Page, and led the lot of them through a finale that threatened to run off the rails, before Lane himself appeared for the encore. The event was a moving demonstration of the affection felt for Lane by his peers and was clearly as enjoyable for the musicians as it was for the audience, because they reassembled in America the following month for a string of nine fund-raising concerts in Dallas, Los Angeles, San Francisco and New York, which led to the establishment of an American branch of ARMS.

While Clapton was playing for the very best of causes, the bread-and-butter business of making money out of his music went on with the release by RSO of a second *Timepieces* compilation of live recordings from the seventies that contained only two previously unissued tracks, followed in 1984 by a two-record retrospective, *Backtrackin'*, which covered his career from 1966 to 1979.

Live appearances in the UK in 1984 were restricted to a tour as Roger Waters' sideman after a crash course in Pink Floyd classics and to an impromptu performance of the closing numbers of Bob Dylan's rousing Wembley Stadium show in July, while fans who wanted to hear new rather than repackaged material were made to wait as Warner Brothers rejected his Phil Collins-produced album for its lack of an obvious hit single, and Collins' subsequent unavailability resulted in another production team, Lenny Waronker and Ted Templeman from the company's Burbank base, recording three new tracks before *Behind The Sun* was released in March 1985.

Warner's concern over Clapton's album was telling. After all they could have allowed him, a respected, established artist, to release the record as fodder for his faithful fans, an extra earner for someone who makes more on the road than in the record racks. That the company wanted hit singles underlines the way rock music and its market have changed since Clapton cut his first track more than twenty years ago. Rock then was youth music exclusively, made for young people of course, and made by them too. Rock itself was barely a decade old and already its early idols were over the hill, even though many, like Elvis Presley, were still in their twenties. The notion that a forty-year-old, as Clapton became on 30 March 1985, might play that kind of music was unthinkable. Yet the generation of performers that emerged with rock's second great explosion in the sixties has survived in significant numbers, supported by an audience which not only includes fans who have grown older with them, but new fans unaware of or unimpressed by earlier achievements. So fans have come to Clapton with each hit of recent years, those who were won over by 'Lay Down Sally' in 1978 or 'Promises' in 1979 or 'I Can't Stand It' in 1981, all top ten US hits, uninterested in comparisons with Cream. And since it's the song essentially that counts, so long as Clapton continues occasionally to snatch one from that secret place inspirational writers have access to, he'll go on having hits that will be heard by new ears. And if they listen hard enough, maybe, just maybe, they'll make out a human hand on a worn fretboard sculpting sounds no synthesizer could create: Eric Clapton's guitar crying like a river of tears, flowing through another year. Unlike some of his gracelessly ageing contemporaries in rock, he can play on as many of his own blues idols have done, just as long as he has the strength to strum and shape a chord.

Discography

Compilation album listings are selective and 'various artists' collections are only listed where Clapton tracks are unavailable elsewhere. (The section containing Clapton's contributions to other artists' recordings makes no claim to chronicle every occasion he sat in on someone else's session.)

The Yardbirds
'I Wish You Would'/'A Certain Girl' (Columbia DB7283, 1964).
'Good Morning Little Schoolgirl'/'I Ain't Got You' (Columbia DB7391, 1964).
'For Your Love'/'Got To Hurry' (Columbia DB7499, 1965).
Five Live Yardbirds (Columbia 33SX1677, 1965; re-released on Charly CR30173, 1979). Too Much Monkey Business/I Got Love If You Want It/ Smokestack Lightnin'/Good Morning Little Schoolgirl/Respectable/ Five Long Years/Pretty Girl/Louise/I'm A Man/Here 'Tis.
Five Yardbirds EP (Columbia seg8421, 1965). My Girl Sloopy/I'm Not Talking/I Ain't Done Wrong.
'Boom Boom'/'Honey In Your Hips' (CBS 1433 – Holland only, 1965).
Sonny Boy Williamson With The Yardbirds (Fontana TL5277, 1966; re-released on Philips 6435.011, 1975, and as part of *Shapes of Things*, Charly BOX 104, 1984). Bye Bye Bird/Mister Downchild/23 Hours Too Long/Out On The Watercoast/Baby Don't Worry/Pontiac Blues/Take It Easy Baby/I Don't Care No More/Do The Weston.
Remember The Yardbirds (EMI Starline SRS 5069, 1971). Heart Full of Soul/Smokestack Lightnin'/I Wish You Would/Good Morning Little Schoolgirl/Evil Hearted You/For Your Love/Shapes Of Things/Still I'm Sad/My Girl Sloopy/A Certain Girl/I Ain't Done Wrong/I'm A Man.
Rock Generation Vol. 1 (BYG 529.701 – France only, 1972). Too Much Monkey Business/Got Love If You Want It/Smokestack Lightnin'/Good Morning Little Schoolgirl/She's So Respectable.
Rock Generation Vol. 2 (BYG 529.702 – France only, 1972). Five Long Years/Pretty Girl/Louise/I'm A Man/Here 'Tis.
Rock Generation Vol. 5 (BYG 529.705 – France only, 1972). Slow Walk/ Yardbirds Beat/My Little Cabin (with Sonny Boy Williamson at Birmingham Town Hall, 1964).
Shapes Of Things (Charly CDX1, 1977). Too Much Monkey Business/I Wish You Would/Good Morning Little Schoolgirl/For Your Love/A Certain Girl/Got To Hurry/Smokestack Lightnin'/Evil Hearted You/

Still I'm Sad/Steeled Blues/Train Kept A Rolling/Here 'Tis/What Do You Want/New York City Blues/For R.S.G./Mr. You're A Better Man Than I/Jeff's Blues/I Ain't Got You/I Ain't Done Wrong/Someone To Love Pts 1 & 2/My Girl Sloopy/Shapes of Things.
The Yardbirds Featuring Eric Clapton (Charly 30194, 1981). For Your Love/I'm A Man/I Wish You Would/Good Morning Little Schoolgirl/A Certain Girl/Got To Hurry/Too Much Monkey Business/Got Love If You Want It/Smokestack Lightnin'/I'm A Man/Here 'Tis.
The Single Hits (Charly CFM 102, 1982). Good Morning Little Schoolgirl/I Ain't Got You/For Your Love/Got To Hurry/Steeled Blues/Heartful Of Soul/Evil Hearted You/Still I'm Sad/Shapes Of Things/You're A Better Man Than I.
Our Own Sound (Charly CFF 7001, 1983). Still I'm Sad/I'm A Man/Evil Hearted You/Steeled Blues/A Certain Girl/I Wish You Would/For Your Love/Heart Full Of Soul/I'm Not Talking/My Girl Sloopy/Got To Hurry.
For Your Love (Topline TOP 103, 1984). For Your Love/Good Morning Little Schoolgirl/I'm A Man/I Wish You Would/A Certain Girl/Got To Hurry/Heartful Of Soul/Shapes Of Things/Steeled Blues/You're A Better Man Than I/Someone To Love Pts 1 & 2.
Shapes Of Things (Charly BOX 104, 1984). A 7-record boxed set containing every Yardbirds recording from 1963–5, including demos, outtakes and alternative versions.

John Mayall and the Bluesbreakers
'I'm Your Witchdoctor'/'Telephone Blues' (Immediate IM012, 1965).

John Mayall with Eric Clapton
Blues Breakers (Decca LK4804, 1966). All Your Love/Hideaway/Little Girl/Another Man/Double Crossing Time/What'd I Say/Key To Love/Parchman Farm/Have You Heard/Ramblin' On My Mind/Steppin' Out/It Ain't Right.

John Mayall and Eric Clapton
'Lonely Years'/'Bernard Jenkins' (Purdah 3502, 1966).

John Mayall with Eric Clapton
'Key To Love'/'Parchman Farm' (Decca F12490, 1966).

Cream
'Wrapping Paper'/'Cat's Squirrel' (Reaction 591007, 1966).
Fresh Cream (Reaction 593001, 1966). NSU/Sleepy Time Time/Dreaming D/Sweet Wine/Spoonful/Cat's Squirrel/Four Until Late/Rollin' And Tumblin'/I'm So Glad/Toad.
'I Feel Free'/'NSU' (Reaction 591011, 1966).
'Strange Brew'/'Tales Of Brave Ulysses' (Reaction 591015, 1967).
Disraeli Gears (Reaction 594003, 1967). Strange Brew/Sunshine Of Your Love/World Of Pain/Dance The Night Away/Blue Condition/Tales Of Brave Ulysses/Swlabr/We're Going Wrong/Outside Woman Blues/Take It Back/Mother's Lament.

'Anyone For Tennis'/'Pressed Rat And Warthog' (Polydor 56358, 1968).
Wheels Of Fire (Polydor 583 031/2, 1968). White Room/Sitting On Top Of
The World/Passing The Time/As You Said/Pressed Rat And Warthog/
Politician/Those Were The Days/Born Under A Bad Sign/Deserted
Cities Of The Heart (Studio Album). Crossroads/Spoonful/Traintime/
Toad (Live At The Fillmore).
Wheels Of Fire (Studio Album) (Polydor 583 033, 1968).
'Sunshine Of Your Love'/'Swlabr' (Polydor 56286, 1968).
Wheels Of Fire (Live At The Fillmore) (Polydor 583 040, 1968).
'White Room'/'Those Were The Days' (Polydor 56300, 1969).
Goodbye (Polydor 583 053, 1969). I'm So Glad/Politician/Sitting On Top
Of The World/Badge/Doing That Scrapyard Thing/What A Bringdown.
'Badge'/'What A Bringdown' (Polydor 56315, 1969).
Best Of Cream (Polydor 583 060, 1969). Sunshine Of Your Love/Badge/
Crossroads/White Room/Swlabr/Born Under A Bad Sign/Spoonful/
Tales Of Brave Ulysses/Strange Brew/I Feel Free.
Live Cream (Polydor 2383 016, 1970). NSU/Sleepy Time Time/Lawdy
Mama/Sweet Wine/Rollin' And Tumblin'.
Live Cream Volume 2 (Polydor 2383 119, 1972). Deserted Cities Of The
Heart/White Room/Politician/Tales Of Brave Ulysses/Sunshine Of Your
Love/Steppin' Out.
Heavy Cream (RSO 2659 022, 1973). Crossroads/White Room/Badge/
Spoonful/Rollin' And Tumblin'/I Feel Free/Born Under A Bad Sign/
Passing The Time/As You Said/Deserted Cities Of The Heart/Cat's
Squirrel/Strange Brew/Sitting On Top Of The World/Swlabr/What A
Bringdown/Tales Of Brave Ulysses/Take It Back/Politician/I'm So
Glad/Sunshine Of Your Love/Those Were The Days/Doing That Scrap-
yard Thing.
Cream (Polydor Standard 2384 067, 1975). NSU/Sleepy Time Time/
Dreaming/Sweet Wine/Spoonful/Wrapping Paper/Cat's Squirrel/Four
Until Late/The Coffee Song/Rollin' And Tumblin'/I'm So Glad/Toad.
Strange Brew – The Very Best Of Cream (RSO RSD 5021, 1983). Badge/
Sunshine Of Your Love/Crossroads/White Room/Born Under A Bad
Sign/Swlabr/Strange Brew/Anyone For Tennis?/I Feel Free/Politician/
Tales Of Brave Ulysses/Spoonful.

Blind Faith
Blind Faith (Polydor 583 059, 1969). Had To Cry Today/Can't Find My
Way Home/Well All Right/Presence Of The Lord/Sea Of Joy/Do What
You Like.

Delaney And Bonnie And Friends
On Tour! Delaney And Bonnie On Tour With Eric Clapton (Atlantic
K30030, 1970). Things Get Better/Poor Elijah/Tribute to Robert John-
son/Only You Know And I Know/I Don't Want To Discuss It/That's
What My Man Is For/Where There's A Will There's A Way/Comin' Home/
Long Tall Sally/Jenny Jenny/The Girl Can't Help It/Tutti Frutti.

Eric Clapton
Eric Clapton (Polydor 2383 021, 1970). Slunky/Bad Boy/Lonesome And A Long Way From Home/After Midnight/Easy Now/Blues Power/Bottle Of Red Wine/Lovin' You Lovin' Me/I've Told You For The Last Time/I Don't Know Why/Let It Rain.

Derek And The Dominos
'Tell The Truth'/'Roll It Over' (Polydor 2058 057, 1970 – withdrawn).

Eric Clapton
'After Midnight'/'Easy Now' (Polydor 2001 096, 1970).

Derek And The Dominos
Layla And Other Assorted Love Songs (Polydor 2625 005, 1970). I Looked Away/Bell Bottom Blues/Keep On Growing/Nobody Knows You (When You're Down And Out)/I Am Yours/Anyday/Key To The Highway/Tell The Truth/Why Does Love Got To Be So Sad/Have You Ever Loved A Woman/Little Wing/It's Too Late/Layla/Thorn Tree In The Garden.
'Layla'/'Bell Bottom Blues' (Polydor 2058 130, 1970 – re-released 1972).
Derek And The Dominos In Concert (RSO 2659 020, 1973). Why Does Love Got To Be So Sad/Tell The Truth/Let It Rain/Presence Of The Lord/Got To Get Better In A Little While/Bottle Of Red Wine/Roll It Over/Blues Power/Have You Ever Loved A Woman.

Eric Clapton
History Of Eric Clapton (Polydor 2659 012, 1972). I Ain't Got You/Hideaway/Tales Of Brave Ulysses/I Want To Know/Sunshine Of Your Love/Crossroads/Sea Of Joy/Only You Know And I Know/I Don't Want To Discuss It/Teasin'/Blues Power/Spoonful/Badge/Tell The Truth/Tell The Truth (jam)/Layla.
Eric Clapton At His Best (RSO 2659 025, 1973). Bottle Of Red Wine/Anyday/I Looked Away/Let It Rain/Lonesome And A Long Way From Home/Sea Of Joy/Layla/Blues Power/Bell Bottom Blues/After Midnight/Keep On Growing/Little Wing/Presence Of The Lord/Why Does Love Got To Be So Sad/Easy Now/Slunky/Key To The Highway.
Eric Clapton's Rainbow Concert (RSO 2394 116, 1973). Badge/Roll It Over/Presence Of The Lord/Pearly Queen/After Midnight/Little Wing.
'I Shot The Sheriff'/'Give Me Strength' (RSO 2090 132, 1974).
461 Ocean Boulevard (RSO 2479 118, 1974). Motherless Children/Give Me Strength/Willie And The Hand Jive/Get Ready/I Shot The Sheriff/I Can't Hold Out/Please Be With Me/Let It Grow/Steady Rollin' Man/Mainline Florida.
'Mainline Florida'/'Willie And The Hand Jive' (RSO 2090 139, 1974).
There's One In Every Crowd (RSO 2479 132, 1975). We've Been Told (Jesus Coming Soon)/Swing Low Sweet Chariot/Little Rachel/Don't Blame Me/The Sky Is Crying/Singin' The Blues/Better Make It Through Today/Pretty Blue Eyes/High/Opposites.
'Swing Low Sweet Chariot'/'Pretty Blue Eyes' (RSO 2090 158, 1975).
The Blues World Of Eric Clapton (Decca SPA 387, 1975). Steppin' Out/

Calcutta Blues/Lonely Years/They Call It Stormy Monday/Shim-Sham-Shimmy/Ramblin' On My Mind/Pretty Girls Everywhere/Hideaway/Key To Love/Bernard Jenkins/Third Degree/Have You Heard.
'Knockin' On Heaven's Door'/'Someone Like You' (RSO 2090 166, 1975).
E. C. Was Here (RSO 2394 160, 1975). Have You Ever Loved A Woman/Presence Of The Lord/Drifting Blues/Can't Find My Way Home/Ramblin' On My Mind/Further On Up The Road.
No Reason To Cry (RSO 2479 179, 1976). Beautiful Thing/Carnival/Sign Language/County Jail Blues/All Our Past Times/Hello Old Friend/Double Trouble/Innocent Times/Hungry/Black Summer Rain.
'Hello Old Friend'/'All Our Past Times' (RSO 2090 208, 1976).
'Carnival'/'Hungry' (RSO 2090 222, 1977).
Slowhand (RSO 2479 201, 1977). Cocaine/Wonderful Tonight/Lay Down Sally/Next Time You See Her/We're All The Way/The Core/May You Never/Mean Old Frisco/Peaches And Diesel.
'Lay Down Sally'/'Cocaine' (RSO 2090 264, 1977).
'Wonderful Tonight'/'Peaches And Diesel' (RSO 2090 275, 1978).
'Promises'/'Watch Out For Lucy' (RSO 21, 1978).
Backless (RSO 5001, 1978). Walk Out In The Rain/Watch Out For Lucy/I'll Make Love To You Anytime/Roll It/Tell Me That You Love Me/If I Don't Be There By Morning/Early In The Morning/Promises/Golden Ring/Tulsa Time.
Clapton (RSO 2479 702, 1978). Willie And The Hand Jive/After Midnight/High/Can't Find My Way Home/Singin' The Blues/Carnival/Blues Power/Motherless Children/Bottle Of Red Wine/Presence Of The Lord.
'If I Don't Be There By Morning'/'Tulsa Time' (RSO 024, 1979).
Just One Night (RSO RSDX 2, 1980). Tulsa Time/Early In The Morning/Lay Down Sally/Wonderful Tonight/If I Don't Be There By Morning/Worried Life Blues/All Our Past Times/After Midnight/Double Trouble/Setting Me Up/Blues Power/Ramblin' On My Mind/Cocaine/Further On Up The Road.
Another Ticket (RSO RSD 5008, 1980). Something Special/Black Rose/Blow Wind Blow/Another Ticket/I Can't Stand It/Hold Me Lord/Floating Bridge/Catch Me If You Can/Rita Mae.
'I Can't Stand It'/'Black Rose' (RSO 74, 1981).
'Another Ticket'/'Rita Mae' (RSO 75, 1981).
Steppin' Out (Decca TAB 21, 1981). Ramblin' On My Mind/Little Girl/All Your Love/Key To Love/Double Crossing Time/Have You Heard/Hideaway/Third Degree/Lonely Years/Pretty Girls Everywhere/Calcutta Blues/Steppin' Out.
'Layla'/'Wonderful Tonight (live)' (RSO 87, 1982).
Timepieces – The Best Of Eric Clapton (RSO RSD 5010, 1982). I Shot The Sheriff/After Midnight/Knockin' On Heaven's Door/Wonderful Tonight/Layla/Cocaine/Lay Down Sally/Willie And The Hand Jive/Promises/Swing Low Sweet Chariot/Let It Grow.
'I Shot The Sheriff'/'Cocaine' (RSO 88, 1982).
'(I've Got A) Rock And Roll Heart'/'Man In Love' (Duck W9780, 1983).
Money And Cigarettes (Duck W3773, 1983). Everybody Oughta Make A Change/The Shape You're In/Ain't Going Down/(I've Got A) Rock And

Roll Heart/Man Overboard/Pretty Girl/Man In Love/Crosscut Saw/Slow
Down Linda/Crazy Country Hop.
'The Shape You're In'/'Crosscut Saw' (Duck W9701, 1983).
Timepieces Vol. II – Live In The Seventies (RSO RSD 5022, 1983). Tulsa
Time/Knockin' On Heaven's Door/If I Don't Be There By Morning/
Ramblin' On My Mind/Presence Of The Lord/Can't Find My Way Home/
Smile/Blues Power.
Backtrackin' (Starblend ERIC 1, 1984). I Shot The Sherriff/Knockin' On
Heaven's Door/Lay Down Sally/Promises/Swing Low Sweet Chariot/
Wonderful Tonight/Sunshine Of Your Love/Tales Of Brave Ulysses/
Badge/Little Wing/Layla/Cocaine/Strange Brew/Let It Rain/Have You
Ever Loved A Woman/Presence Of The Lord/Crossroads/Roll It Over/
Can't Find My Way Home/Blues Power/Further On Up The Road.
'Wonderful Tonight'/'Cocaine' (RSO 98, 1984).
'Forever Man'/'Too Bad' (Warner Bros. W9069, 1985).
Behind The Sun (Warner Bros. K9251661, 1985). She's Waiting/See What
Love Can Do/Same Old Blues/Knock On Wood/Something's Happening/
Forever Man/It All Depends/Tangled In Love/Never Make You Cry/Just
Like A Prisoner/Behind The Sun.

Various Artists Compilations
History Of British Blues (Sire SAS 3701) – 'Baby What's Wrong' (from
Yardbirds' first demo session in February 1964); *Blues Anytime Vol 1*
(Immediate IMLP 014) – 'Snake Drive', 'Tribute To Elmore', 'West Coast
Idea', (plus 'I'm Your Witchdoctor' and 'Telephone Blues' with John
Mayall and the Bluesbreakers); *Blues Anytime Vol 3* (Immediate IMLP
019) – 'Miles Road'; *An Anthology Of British Blues Vol 1* (Immediate
IMAL 03/4) – 'Freight Loader', 'Choker' (plus 'Snake Drive' and 'Tribute
To Elmore'); *Happy To Be Part Of The Industry Of Human Happiness*
(Immediate IMLYIN 2) – 'On Top Of The World', (plus 'Tribute to
Elmore'); *What's Shakin'* (Elektra EKS 74002) – 'I Want To Know',
'Crossroads', 'Steppin' Out' (as Eric Clapton and the Powerhouse).

Records by other artists
'Mean Old World'/Duane Allman (on *An Anthology*, Capricorn K67502);
The Last Waltz/The Band (Warner Bros K66076); *The Beatles*/The
Beatles (Apple PMC 7067); 'Teasin''/King Curtis (Atco 2400 106); *Jesse
Ed Davis*/Jesse Ed Davis (Atlantic 2400 106); *The Sun Moon & Herbs*/Dr
John The Night Tripper (Atlantic 2400 161); *From New Orleans to
Chicago*/Champion Jack Dupree (Decca LK 4747); *Lady Soul*/Aretha
Franklin (Atlantic 587099); *Buddy Guy And Junior Wells Play The Blues*/
Buddy Guy And Junior Wells (Atlantic K40240); *Wonderwall*/George
Harrison (Apple SAPCOR 1); *All Things Must Pass*/George Harrison
(Apple STCH 639); *Concert For Bangla Desh*/George Harrison and
others (Apple STCX 3385); *George Harrison*/George Harrison (Dark
Horse K56562); *The London Sessions*/Howlin' Wolf (Rolling Stones COC
49101); *Sometime In New York City*/John Lennon (Apple SVBB3392); *Is
This What You Want*/Jackie Lomax (Apple SAPCOR 6); 'Knockin' On
Heaven's Door'/Arthur Louis (Plum PIP 001); *Back To The Roots*/John

Mayall (Polydor 2425 062/3); *We're Only In It For The Money*/Mothers Of Invention (Verve VLP 9199); *Music From Free Creek* (Charisma ADS 1/2); 'Cold Turkey'/Plastic Ono Band (Apple 1001); *Live Peace In Toronto – 1969*/Plastic Ono Band (Apple CORE 2001); *That's The Way God Planned It*/Billy Preston (Apple SAPCOR 9); *Leon Russell*/Leon Russell (A&M AMLS 982); 'Labio-Dental Fricative'/Viv Stansall's Sean Head Showband (Liberty LBF 15309); *Stephen Stills*/Stephen Stills (Atlantic 2401 004); *Rough Mix*/Pete Townshend and Ronnie Lane (Polydor 2442 147); *Doris Troy*/Doris Troy (Apple SAPCOR 13); *Friends And Angels*/ Martha Velez (London SHK 8395); *The Pros And Cons Of Hitch Hiking*/ Roger Waters (Harvest SHVL 24 0105); *Tommy* (film soundtrack)/The Who and others (Polydor 2335 093/4); *Lumpy Gravy*/Frank Zappa (Verve VLP 9223).

INDEX